M000211059

Whatever You Do, Don't Run

*True stories and reflections by
not-so-rugged rangers*

DAVID HOOD, JAMES HENDRY,
CHRIS ROCHE & MEGAN EMMETT

Tafelberg

Tafelberg
an imprint of NB Publishers
40 Heerengracht, Cape Town, 8000
www.tafelberg.com
© text 2006 authors

All rights reserved
No part of this book may be reproduced or transmitted in any form
or by any electronic or mechanical means, including photocopying
and recording, or by any other information storage or retrieval system,
without written permission from the publisher

© drawings and photographs:
Dave Hood – pp 21, 23, 25, 31, 51, 53, 56, 57, 62, 68, 95, 125, 131, 152, 164
Chris Roche – pp 5, 77, 110, 111, 114, 115, 118, 120, 122, 140, 145, 154
Megan Emmett – pp 3, 15, 18, 28, 37, 42, 45, 49, 58, 59, 74, 79, 82, 89, 96,
108, 156, 159, 168, 169, 173, 180, 181

Set in Galliard
Cover design by Dorét Fereirra of Dotted Line Design based on photographs by
Guy Stubbs (man) and Megan Emmett (buffalo and elephant)
Book design by Nazli Jacobs
Edited by James Woodhouse
Proofread by Linéll van Hoepen

Printed and bound by Paarl Print, Oosterland Street, Paarl, South Africa
First edition, first printing 2006
Fifth printing 2009

ISBN 13: 978-0-624-04424-6

Acknowledgements

Theologians and scientists are still fighting amongst themselves, trying to establish how it all happened, how we ended up on this world full of beautiful creatures. I would like to acknowledge the Great Creator – however He did it – because it is thanks to Him that we have anything to write about at all. I would also like to thank Catherine, without whose help and support I would never have had the courage to carry this project through. – *Dave*

My gratitude to all who I have worked with in wild southern Africa. I have been lucky enough to work with some amazing people and have learnt something from everyone about so many different facets of nature and life. – *Chris*

Thank you: Elvis, Chris, Mike, Graham, Dave, Alex, Derrick, Dyke and Johnson. Yours is the legacy that will continue to build this great continent. – *James*

I'd like to thank every person I've encountered along my journey of becoming a 'ranger' who has provided opportunity, resource, support, education and inspiration to me and so facilitated my childhood dream come true. The list is a long one. – *Megan*

The Job Description

A ranger or field guide is responsible for all aspects of hosting a group of guests during their stay at a safari lodge, from ensuring their safety when in the bush to having an evening meal with them or chatting around the fire. The overall aim is to open a window onto the natural world and to allow guests to enter it at their own pace. This includes taking them on game walks and drives and educating them on every aspect of nature from insects, birds, mammals and bats to plants, grasses, soils and stars. A good guide will cover as many disciplines as possible during the guests' often short stay but will focus on their own special interests. A bad guide will focus on the Big Five. When not responsible for guests, a ranger's duties include shooting practice, basic land management (alien vegetation eradication, road clearing, erosion control and the like), monitoring and research projects and helping to train other rangers. A ranger may on occasion be called upon to perform an almost endless list of other tasks, from maintaining vehicles to capturing animals.

A Ranger's Day

An unwelcome bleeping shatters the peaceful bushveld night. I reach over in the dark, fumbling for the offensive alarm clock and send it clattering to the floor. Stretching for the bedside light, I flick the switch, locate the electronic racket and push the off-button. It is 05h00, very dark and a bit chilly.

I calculate quickly that I have had five hours' sleep since the two Dutch couples I was entertaining last night finally left the fireside and went to bed. This is their last morning and I know they still haven't seen the lion they so desperately want to see. I feel a knot forming in my stomach, knowing that no lions have been seen during the last week. In all likelihood, they are on parts of their territory that fall outside of our concession. My guests have such high hopes . . . I feel daunted by the challenge of finding these elusive creatures before we have to return to the lodge at 09h30 for a quick breakfast and a 10h30 departure in the Cessna 210 scheduled to pick them up at the reserve's airstrip.

Stumbling drowsily into the shower, I think of the times when the lodge has been quieter and I have been able to spend time in the bush by myself, tracking animals or training new rangers. Even the hard work of clearing overgrown bush from sandy roads seems preferable to the task facing me now.

At 05h25, I am at the lodge building in my newly polished boots. I check that the morning tea and coffee table has been set up correctly for the guests before gulping down a strong cup of Kenya's finest myself. Other rangers start to appear and we chat briefly before joining our guests with as much enthusiasm as we can muster.

By 06h10 we are all on the Land Rover and on the lookout for lions. I am all too aware that the great cats may escape us and point out other interesting animals and birds along the way, at the same time entertaining my charges with a few choice snippets of natural history.

We make it back to the lodge at 09h45 and I am forced to urge the guests to hurry their breakfast before we have to leave for the airstrip in half an hour. We had a brief glimpse of a lioness on the drive and although the guests are delighted, I feel the sighting was far too rushed. I wave goodbye to the little aircraft as it wobbles on the warming air.

Back at the lodge I check the notice board for the afternoon's activities. It is not my turn to take the morning walk so I return to my room for an hour's nap before lunch.

After lunch I sit for a while in the ranger's room, watching one of the trainees clean his rifle while chatting to another guide about his holiday plans for the Mozambican coast.

At 14h30, I am feeling decidedly sleepy and return to my room hoping to squeeze in a short half-hour nap before the afternoon drive.

Less than an hour later, I find myself once again at the lodge, this time waiting for my new guests to come down for tea. I am always a little apprehensive at this time, wondering what the new arrivals will be like. The American family designated to me arrived at the lodge just after lunch and have already been welcomed and settled into their chalets. They turn out to be friendly and easy to get along with. After fielding a few rather bizarre questions about the local wildlife, I show them a map of the reserve and go through a thorough orientation, explaining the safety regulations, the layout of the reserve, our daily schedule and something of the area's history.

We have a fantastic drive and, unhurried by the pressure of time, we are able to spend time watching a herd of elephants cavorting and splattering themselves with mud at a drying pan. After dark we begin to head back to the lodge, using a spotlight to spot an owl and a chameleon. Close to the lodge we even catch a brief glimpse of a serval.

Back at camp, I leave my exhilarated guests with the security guards who will walk them safely back to their luxury chalets. We have agreed that the guards will fetch them at 20h00, giving them half an hour to freshen up before dinner. Tired but energised by a good drive, I lock my rifle in the safe and return to my own, rather more basic room for a quick shower, ridding myself of the day's dust and sweat.

At dinner, I host the group, recommending one of the lodge's pinotages with their ostrich steak. After coffee, the Americans, probably tired from travelling and the excitement of the drive, decline my offer of drinks around the fire, leaving me free to return wearily to my bed.

Thus ends another day as a ranger.

DAVID HOOD

Table of Contents

Introduction, 13

Tree Hugger – *David Hood*, 15
Lost in Translation, 22
Take a Walk – on the Wild Side – *David Hood*, 23
Fear – A Rock Star in the Wilderness? – *James Hendry*, 31
Super-spectral Vision, 44
Girls Just Wanna Have Fun – *Megan Emmett*, 45
Nocturnal Vision, 51
Tracker – *James Hendry*, 53
Firewood and Elephant Nests, 67
Whatever You Do, Don't Run! – *David Hood*, 68
Guests Say the Darnedest Things, 76
Monstrous Mammals – *David Hood*, 77
Lend Me Your Ears, 87
The Rules – *David Hood*, 89
Seventeen Years in Brothels, 100
Snake Stories: Silly, Serious and Sublime – *Chris Roche*, 101
Birding – *James Hendry*, 108
The Whites of Their Eyes, 123
Things that Go *Bump* in the Night – *Megan Emmett*, 125
Crutches and Lions, 130
The Puff Adder and the Hyaena – *David Hood*, 131
Heavy Summer Eyes, 138
In Search of the Ornithological Grail – *Chris Roche*, 140
Careful with my Corvette, 144
Bushpilots! – *David Hood*, 145
Safety in Colours, 154

Another Story – *David Hood*, 156
All in a Day's Work – *Megan Emmett*, 169
The Ancient Truth – *James Hendry*, 176

Nomenclature, 187

About the Authors, 195

Introduction

The stories that you read in this book are all real-life accounts written by rangers who have worked, and, in some cases, still do work, in game reserves in southern Africa. We all concur that the days of the rugged, gung ho ranger are over – or at least that they should be. Many of the practices of the 'fearless' ranger were founded either on ignorance or, in an endeavour to display their own bravado, on a desire to instil fear in the people they were with. Without doubt these foolhardy attempts caused undue stress to the animals involved.

Nevertheless, wild places still exist and wild animals still consider man a threat. The relationships with the wilderness that the four of us possess have grown from journeys of fear, disillusionment, frustration, discovery and awe – and, of course, from insect bites. In the past we have crossed human-animal boundaries that we would now consider disrespectful; we have blundered about the bush causing damage to flora and disruption to fauna. Yet, we have honestly related those incidences to you, the reader, in the hope that you will learn from our experiences rather than judge us by them.

Once, we too considered the thrill of the bush to be a charge by an enraged elephant bull or an encounter with a lion on foot. Now we know there is a much greater thrill to be found in the discovery and study of that astonishing mosaic of life, death, earth and water that we so casually sum up with one word: 'nature'.

We hope you will enjoy our stories, but know that the real wonder is not to be found on these pages but in the patterns on an insect's thorax, the shimmer of a bird's wings, the faithfulness of a jackal, the testament of old bones and the knowledge that these few things are part of just one circle of life amidst a magnificent yet unfathomable current of interrelatedness.

The Authors

Tree Hugger – My first Trail

(On the banks of the Umfolozi)

by DAVID HOOD

The wilderness trail can be a terrifying experience for the uninitiated. Leaving the vehicles at the side of the road and wandering off into bush teeming with lions, rhinoceroses, snakes and spiders does not come naturally to most. The realisation that the heavy pack on your back does not contain even the small luxury of a tent is also not comforting. The undeniable fact that you are carrying a sleeping mat is convincing evidence that maybe they were serious when they suggested the surely suicidal act of 'sleeping out'. The fact that they gilded it so delightfully with descriptions of the stars overhead and a big fire close at hand only serves to reinforce the unsettling notion that perhaps beautiful thatched bungalows won't miraculously appear out of nowhere accompanied by the ranger's raucous laugh and welcome rhetoric: 'What, you really thought I'd make you sleep out?'

Yet, as terrifying as this experience may seem, it can be nothing short of life-changing for its quivering participants. The conversion of irrational fear into a soul's undeniable resonance with nature is no small miracle. Few trailists would consider that any mechanism other than a mighty, all-knowing God was behind the wonders around them. And, as quickly as these experiences are forgotten in the hustle and bustle of everyday life, they seldom fail to inscribe themselves indelibly on the inner beings of those who have participated in a real wilderness trail.

Sometimes I rely on the memory of these experiences to help me through long days with disinterested or jaded guests. My first trail gave me an insight into the raw power of nature and the influence it has on people, myself among them. The belief that some guests may go home

15

with something of the experience I had, helps me to tolerate the consistent fourteen-hour days without weekends, the ludicrous salary, the problems with the neglected accommodation and the fights with the kitchen staff. It also helps me to face down proclamations from euphoric guests that I have the perfect job and live in paradise without being spurious in my returns.

Leaving the air-conditioned vehicles at the side of the road we strapped the last pots and sleeping mats onto our rucksacks. We were ten in all, led by a long-haired, unshaven ranger in his late thirties with a penchant for Chris Rea and Winston cigarettes. He was a man of few words but appeared verbose next to his one-eyed Zulu tracker. Then there was us, the rabble – seven snotty-nosed, know-it-all, high-school boys. Overseeing us was our Geography teacher, the only female in our group, who, in hindsight, must have been a remarkably tolerant person. She was a young teacher, young enough at heart to get thoroughly stuck into the experience as much as any of us.

To start, we wound our way along well-used game trails through sparse *Acacia* woodland, wary of every stump and hillock. It wasn't long before the vast Umfolozi riverbed spread itself out before our animal-hungry eyes. As we made our way down towards the dense reeds on the edge of the riverbed, both ranger and tracker unshouldered their rifles, whose bullets – as we had already seen – resembled artillery shells more than hunting rounds. We looked at the big weapons held at the ready and then turned and grinned at one another, hoping to find reassurance from the uncertain excitement we were all feeling. We were later to learn that these reedbeds were a favourite haunt of old buffalo bulls.

Soon after having crossed the white sand of the riverbed we made our first camp. Here, to our amazement, were a couple of canvass structures that vaguely resembled human shelters. Although they were open on one side, and not nearly big enough to accommodate our group, their presence was comforting. Were they breaking us in gently? Certainly they were the last evidence of humanity we were to see for the next four days.

After a dinner cooked on the fire in the big aluminium pot, we planned the night watch. In groups of two we were to take two-hour shifts to keep the fire going and protect the camp from marauding wildlife. In our minds, I think we were all planning exactly what action we would take if marauding wildlife of some sort did take an interest in our camp. Time would reveal that the most common course of action in this event was to run to Bruce, the snoring ranger, wake him up and hastily describe the shapes advancing in the flickering firelight. His response became predictable – he would ask after the colour of its eyes before rolling over and going back to sleep, leaving the disillusioned boys to face the terror alone and unaided.

The first night nothing came into our camp but, lying on my rollup foam mattress and staring through the scraggly branches above me at the stars, I heard a sound.

'What's that?' came the alarmed enquiry from a nearby sleeping bag.

'Lions,' replied our ranger nonchalantly.

I had had the privilege of visiting a number of game reserves before and I had also slept out on many mountain trails, but I had never before combined the two. This was the fulfilment of a dream and I must have fallen asleep with a smile on my face. I certainly slept soundly between guard duties.

The next morning, I awoke refreshed and ready for the day's adventures. My enthusiasm was soon tempered by confusion – something was wrong in the camp, something was different. Nerves had been frayed and some of my fellow trailists had not slept much or at all. I was taken aback. My schoolboy associates were truly shaken and this unexpected fear and uncertainty was most pronounced in those individuals who had always oozed confidence, particularly in the sporting arena. What had happened to them I wondered – weren't they supposed to be the tough guys? In one bushveld night, egos had been destroyed, status had been obliterated and perceptions rearranged.

Slightly subdued I helped clean the camp. We buried the fire and then, breaking leafy branches, we swept away our footprints so that no trace of our passing was left. Then we set off into the unknown. We had nothing here, not even our self-assuredness, to lean on – we were starting from scratch.

Through our experiences on the four-night trail we learnt a humble respect for one another and we saw many things; most notable of these were the rhino, lots of rhino. On one day we counted just over thirty rhino – both black and white – an impressive tally. The cool mornings were when we did most of our walking and game viewing, usually followed by a shorter afternoon walk. During the heat of the day we would dig for water in the riverbed, filling our bottles before retiring to the shade of a Sycamore Fig or *Acacia* tree to laze away the early afternoon. Some in our group were quick to discover that a big chunk of rhino dung made an excellent substitute for a rugby ball, and with the Umfolozi as our field we would play touch rugby in the cool evenings. As one rugby ball shattered into a spray of grassy chunks, another could always be found to replace it. But it was the evenings that captured our imaginations. Thick-tailed bushbabies would bounce about in the trees above us and the eerie calls of hyaena would emanate from somewhere beyond the firelight. It was then that we could contemplate man's chang-

ing place among other living things, and then that we could feel that no man was better off than we were, sitting around the fire that we had built and cooked upon.

One night I decided to stay up after dinner to complete my diary entry before retiring for a short sleep prior to night watch later that evening. As I was finishing noting down the day's events, a rhino approached the camp. Their presence always made us feel extraordinarily vulnerable, especially on the flat terrain where we were camped. On the first occasion, the rhino did not stay for long before melting back into the shadows, but later, during our watch, a second rhino appeared who was more curious. Its eyes remained in the torchlight as it shuffled uneasily back and forth and huffed at us.

My companion began to fear for his life. 'What shall we do?' he asked.

'I'm not sure, maybe we should shine the torch in its eyes until it goes away.'

The rhino did not comply but kept shuffling around in the shadows.

'Do you think it's coming closer?' I asked.

'I don't know, should I go and call Bruce?' he replied, hesitant to wake the unsympathetic ranger.

'I don't know, if you want.' The rhino shuffled once more.

'I'm going to wake him!' he said, and disappeared into the darkness while I shone the torch at the blinking lights of the rhino's eyes. Moments later he returned from the shadows with this report: 'He asked me what the colour of its eyes were and then went back to sleep, I couldn't wake him again . . .'

'I think it's gone,' I replied. 'Can you see anything?'

We scanned the area regularly but saw no further sign of the grey beast. Eventually it was time to wake the next watch and we could hand over the responsibility of the camp's safety and return to our sleeping bags.

The following morning I discovered that we had not been the only watch to see large animals in the night. A later watch had had an encounter with a Spotted Hyaena. There had been three boys on watch – two on official duty and a third who couldn't sleep. When the hyaena began its fearless approach, one of them had grabbed a flaming branch out of the fire. He had held it in terror as the hyaena approached to within a few metres. They laughed as they described how the torch-bearer had held the branch upright, not noticing as burning pieces of it fell onto his boots.

On another occasion we were lucky enough to see a pride of lions. We had just struck camp and the afternoon heat was beginning to dissipate. It was still hot though and Bruce permitted three of the boys to go for a swim in a nearby waterhole. We had passed the waterhole on the way to camp and it had been declared crocodile free by our guide. I found it amazing that crocodiles could withstand the long dry periods of this seasonal river by simply aestivating under riverbanks or moving between miniscule waterholes.

While they went for a swim, and to replenish our water supplies, the rest of us climbed to the top of a nearby krantz from where we could see another beautiful stretch of the dry Umfolozi's white sand. We scanned the area below us picking up impala and Common Waterbuck. Our ancient tracker who appeared to take very little notice of what was going on around him tilted his head back slightly so that he could peer off into the distance with his one good, but slightly squint, eye. He pointed down the riverbed and mumbled something incomprehensible. We turned to Bruce for a translation.

'He says there are lions over there.'

After a good few minutes of geographical descriptions and binocular scanning, we had all spotted, with our advanced optical equipment, what the old Zulu had spotted with a single squint eye. Even after seeing the shapes moving onto the sand of the riverbed, it took a few more moments for us all to concur that they were in fact lions – so far away were they. We watched them ambling slowly in our direction for some time before considering that if they kept going they would meet our friends swimming naked in the waterhole. We could not see the waterhole from where we were, nor was it within shouting distance so we dispatched one of our number to go and warn them.

It took little persuasion to convince them that they should return to camp. There we met the breathless group from the waterhole, obviously relieved to be back in camp and laughing hysterically. Apparently they had not waited to see where the lions were but had taken the messenger's word for it. It seemed that trying to don underpants while sprinting up a hill, laden with water bottles, in the face of an advancing pride of lions had reduced them to riotous mirth!

We settled into the by now ritual activity of cooking the evening meal, enjoying the late afternoon sounds only so far as our ravenous stomachs would let us think about anything other than food. As the aroma of dinner mingled with the scent of the wood fire we waited hungrily.

Barely had the delicious meal been dished up onto our eagerly offered plates – I had just begun to look for a comfortable rock to sit on – when the cry went up: 'There's a rhino – run!'

Bodies evacuated the camp, scrambling up boulders behind our little clearing and into nearby trees. I did not actually see the rhino, but the actions of those around me were enough to convince me. I made a dash for the nearest tree only to find that I was not the first one there. A fellow student was hoisting himself frantically up the tree with his dinner still in one hand. I willed him to move faster and then clambered up the slightly angled trunk behind him, almost dropping my plate in the process. Having scrambled up the tree high enough to be out of horn's reach, I hugged the tree with one hand, balanced my dinner in the other and searched the surrounds for any sign of the offending pachyderm. I never did see the rhino which had apparently been 'just over there'; nonetheless, the glimpse that had sent us all scattering into the trees was enough to convince us to stay and eat dinner in our chosen refuges.

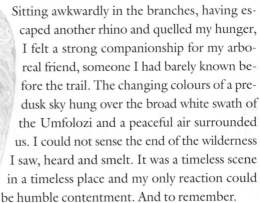

Sitting awkwardly in the branches, having escaped another rhino and quelled my hunger, I felt a strong companionship for my arboreal friend, someone I had barely known before the trail. The changing colours of a pre-dusk sky hung over the broad white swath of the Umfolozi and a peaceful air surrounded us. I could not sense the end of the wilderness I saw, heard and smelt. It was a timeless scene in a timeless place and my only reaction could be humble contentment. And to remember.

Lost in Translation

I am reminded of the of story some Italian guests who could not speak English and whose guide could speak no Italian. The guests enthusiastically lapped up everything Dumi had to say, but on a walk he hit a blank when trying to explain what giraffe dung was. Using the actual pellets, he graphically tried to demonstrate the fact that the dung was the result of leaves being ingested and then passed through the animal's digestive system. When the guests promptly popped some into their mouths and began to chew with some gusto, he realised that, despite their enthusiasm, they had not understood.

Chris Roche

Take a Walk – on the Wild Side

(High up in a Marula Tree)

by DAVID HOOD

'**P**art of our training involves walking the reserve's roads to get to know them better,' I explained, passing the silver butter dish across the table.

Amanda took a rather larger gulp of red wine than I think she intended. Light from the paraffin lamp flickered across her face as she set her crystal wine glass down. 'Why can't you just drive them?' she asked.

'You get to know them more intimately if you walk and you have time to memorise features along the way, like special trees or odd-looking termite mounds. You are able to memorise road junctions far more effectively and that all helps when you need to give directions to another ranger or come out of a block onto a road and you're not exactly sure where you are. When you drive, you miss a lot.'

Arnold, another of the four guests at the table, toyed with a pork medallion and then asked, 'But you're armed, right?'

The obvious question, it unwittingly laid bare a plethora of misconceptions about the African wilderness. It could be answered in such a way as to reinforce those misconceptions, keeping fear and dependence alive and ensuring for myself the position of all-knowing, SUPREME RANGER. Or it could be used as a window to a brave attempt at the truth.

I had a clumsy go at the latter: 'A rifle is not as necessary as you may think. It is usually only used as a last resort and even so, things often happen so fast that there is not even time to use it. It is far better to avoid any potential situations. Even if you have a rifle, I believe that you should act as though you do not.

'Besides, learning the roads is only part of the purpose of the walks. They are also intended to improve a ranger's awareness. Without a rifle, you feel a lot more vulnerable, you don't take chances and you look around you a lot more. We are given a hand-held radio, so we can call for help if we really need it.'

I fitted in half a baby corn before the next question.

Amanda again: 'But what if you come across a lion or an elephant – what then?'

I realised that my answer had missed the mark. Perhaps a more oblique approach would be more effective. I decided to tell them a story. I reached for my neglected glass of whisky and thought back to my training days . . .

It was a bleak morning, good weather for walking the thirty kilometres or so of roads that we had on the agenda for that day. Due to a shortage of radios and an excess of trainees, we were doing the walks in two groups of two. Initially I was disappointed that I would not be able to do them alone, but when I was designated Brent as a companion, it didn't seem too bad – he was good company.

Brent and I were ambitious, we had a total of nine days of walking which we were part way through and we had already established the best way of doing it. We would wake up well before first light, throw on appropriate attire and head for the kitchen. There an enormous bowl of cereal would be speedily guzzled. Brent generally settled for a salad bowl as the normal soup bowls just weren't quite big enough.

One of us would clip the first-aid kit, packed into a moonbelt, around his waist while the other would be responsible for the radio. Our remaining hands would be filled with at least one bottle of water (two if it looked like it was going to be really hot) and some fruit. We knew we could dig for water in the riverbed or drink at a muddy waterhole if we got desperate. We did not bother with the recommended day pack filled with sandwiches, binoculars, cooldrink et cetera, reasoning that it would only slow us down.

We each had a grubby map, which would be folded and tucked into a pocket. Our strategy was to walk most of the route hard and fast. We would stop to look at interesting things but always planned to be back just after lunch. On returning to the little camp, we would sit down for a challenge of computer-simulated bird identification in the form of 'Robert's Bird Games' while downing two ice-cold Cokes, one after the other. This would all be accomplished between wolfing down large portions of any lunch that the guests had left.

Since our strategy worked well and allowed for an afternoon nap, we stuck to it regimentally. On the morning in question, we set out amidst a gloomy pre-dawn glow. The sun rose somewhere, but the shifty grey masses that drifted overhead hid it from view. That was a pity because the sun would help us a great deal if we got lost. As compensation, we noted carefully the wind direction and hoped it would be a steady, reliable compass. To begin with, we tried to talk little, absorbing our surroundings and doing our best to spot animals, birds, tracks and useful landmarks.

Walking has a way of releasing the imagination and after an hour or two, Brent and I had lapsed into subdued conversation, punctuated with long periods of thoughtful silence. A good distance into our walk, the grey shapes overhead began to shower us with a gentle drizzle. We adjusted our pace a little to stay warm. We kept going, putting kilometre after kilometre behind us.

It must have been around mid-morning when we came upon a leopard track. It was a beautiful, clear track in the mud next to a puddle. It was fresh too – it had blotted out the surrounding pockmarks etched by the recent rainfall. We studied it carefully. The oval toes and the natural curves of the pad radiated a tangible presence. We knew that only a few moments in time separated us and the leopard. Perhaps it had even seen us coming and moved away before we had spotted it.

We searched the ground for more tracks and finding others we worked out that it had been walking along the road in the same direction as we were headed. Shortly after the first track that we had seen, it had left the road on the left hand side, which was also the western side. What a pity we had not seen it. Perhaps it was close. Maybe it was watching us!

We decided to track it. We were not by any stretch experienced trackers and leopard are one of the hardest animals to track, but we decided: why not try. We set off in the direction it had left the road, scrutinising the barer patches of soil on game paths for the rounded edges of its pads. We found more tracks near the road and one further away, but after that we struggled.

We looked all over, knowing that there must be more signs – if only we could see them! In our search for more prints, Brent and I drifted apart. I could still see him through the gaps between leafy bushwillows and was doing my best to keep an eye on where he was while at the same time studying the ground for tracks. The problem was that the game paths along which the leopard might have walked were not clear in this area. The ground was hard and the paths were overgrown – not a good place to find footprints.

I decided to stick with the trail I was on and go a bit further ahead, maybe the ground would be softer. I would not go far and then I would come back and find Brent. I continued along the path, concentrating hard, trying to see tracks. When at last I looked up, it was not a leopard I saw, but a pride of lions.

My breath caught in my throat. I crouched down immediately, trying to make myself less obvious. There were five of them and they were lying about on the edge of a small rain-filled pan. They had not seen me so I watched them for a moment.

I could see a male clearly. I could see his big mane, his round ears and his hunter's eyes. They were not looking in my direction. The small pride was about a hundred metres away. I was not afraid but I was very excited at having seen them and wanted Brent to see right away.

o where the bush was thicker before standing up
or Brent from there, not wanting to lose sight of
raid of losing sight of them in case they smelt or
ed – I would be happier knowing exactly where

a little way off, I whispered as loudly as I could,
'P   dn't hear my call and continued walking away.
I f   as leading me steadily away from where the
lion   nt!' I tried again but he kept walking. I wanted to   t knew that moving fast through thick bush
would   noise. I clicked my fingers together, hoping tha   ound that would not unduly disturb the
lions, n   ce away. Finally, that got Brent's attention
and I wa   inting in the direction that I had seen the
lions. I explained in a whisper that I had seen the lions and led the
way back towards the pan. When we got beyond the trees that
blocked our view of the little waterhole, we saw the lions. They
were looking at us. All of them!

I was angry with myself because I knew I had made too much
noise trying to get Brent's attention. It was always a pity to disturb animals unnecessarily. And now we had five lions to deal with.

There was mostly open ground between them and us. Our gazes
cut across it like knives. Theirs cut back. We felt suddenly very exposed. I had seen lions on foot before and my experiences led me
to believe that we were not in any immediate danger. Brent was
not so sure and got his Leatherman out – just in case.

The lions, after a brief examination, turned and moved into
thicker bush behind the pan. Four of them disappeared completely
but the male came out again, moving to the right. We started to
back away too, in the direction of the road. As we went we could
see that the male was moving at an angle that would bring him
closer to us. He was not focused on us – although I am quite sure
he was well aware of exactly where we were – he was simply moving in a certain direction that would lead him to a certain place.

We changed our direction slightly so that we would not get any closer, while still keeping a watchful eye on his progress. He was more than a hundred metres away now and we could only see him intermittently through gaps in the bush. Then the bush got thicker, he walked behind a tree and never came out. We walked on, hoping to catch sight of him again.

When we hadn't seen him for a while – which may have only been a few moments – we decided to climb a tree. Perhaps we would see him and the other lions from a higher vantage point. Nearby was a large marula tree with a fork low down that we could clamber onto. One at a time we hoisted ourselves up and then climbed higher among the tree's thick branches.

It was autumn and the marulas had lost most of their leaves, giving us a clear view out over the surrounding bush. Unfortunately the smaller bushwillows still clung to their green and yellow foliage and we were unable to spot the lions amongst them. We waited, hoping that they would walk through an open patch where we could catch a glimpse of their regal confidence but after a few minutes realised that this was not going to happen. Never mind: we had had a good look already.

We lay around like leopards in the big marula tree, enjoying the view and resting legs weary from the morning's walk and the previous days of hard slogging. It was peaceful up there and we talked a little between listening to the sounds of the bush and gazing out across the sea of autumn colour below us. The excitement provided by the lions was soon replaced by a comfortable lethargy. The thought of many kilometres still to walk did little to energise us.

I paused in the telling of my story, looked at the guests trying to gauge their reaction and took another sip of whisky. I hoped that by now they would be starting to understand that lions are not as malicious as they had presumed.

A waiter cleared the guests' plates and looked questioningly at me as mine was still half full. I had been doing a lot of talking. 'You can take my plate, thank you, mfo*,' I told him.

Something grunted overhead and everyone looked up at the stars. 'It's a baboon,' I explained, 'probably on the thatch roof.'

Concerned gazes relaxed and another guest, Lucas, who hadn't said much turned to me, 'So you're up a tree with lions prowling nearby – what did you do next?'

'Actually we weren't worried about the lions anymore,' I replied, hammering another nail into the coffin of unreasonable lion phobia, 'but something else did happen before we continued our walk.'

We had been lazing in the tree just long enough to feel new energy seeping back into our weary legs, when we heard the sound of a vehicle. It seemed to be coming our way.

Now one of our strict instructions on these walks was that we were not to be spotted by anyone. We had already done our share of last-minute dashes into the bush, scrambling behind low bushes and watching oblivious vehicles rumble past. We had the cuts and scrapes to prove it.

Only once had we been caught out. It was a long, straight road and we had not heard the vehicle. They spotted us at a distance. We immediately ran for cover but the ranger driving took this as a personal challenge. With engine whining and guests holding onto their caps, he came charging after us. We ran hard but soon heard the vehicle turning off the road where we had left it. We guessed by the raucous exclamations that we could hear that he and his guests were having a lot of fun at our expense. All the more reason

* Brother

not to let him find us again! It sounded as though he told his tracker to go and find us. We continued to run, zig-zagging, jumping over roads and doing anything that we imagined would throw a good tracker off our trail. Eventually we returned cautiously to the road we had left and were relieved to find no sign of our pursuers.

Not wishing to repeat the experience from our present position, we assessed the situation. Our choice of tree had been particularly bad. Our comfortable marula was less than twenty metres from a bend in the track we were supposed to be following. We were in a very exposed position.

It had been a fairly precarious climb to get to where we were and we would not have time to get back down before the vehicle came by. We could jump, or we could stay frozen to the tree trunks and hope they didn't notice us. We quickly discussed our options while studying the tough bushes and hard ground six or seven metres below. Unanimously we dismissed jumping and unanimously we imitated leopards sprawling invisibly on the marula's substantial boughs – only, we lacked the camouflage.

Trying not to move our heads, we watched with trepidation as the vehicle, loaded to the brim with humanity, approached our tree. It wound its way steadily along the sand track. By the time it drew level with us, no one had seen us, they seemed to all be looking at the road or not looking at all. Then one observant soul – confound him – looked up and let out an alarm call.

The vehicle stopped and a myriad of heads swung up to gape at our khaki-clad figures. We grinned foolishly and the vehicle reversed. They greeted us bemusedly. 'There are lions over there and we wanted to see if we could see them from up here,' I explained and everyone in the vehicle turned to look in the direction of my outstretched arm. Of course there was nothing to see.

Fear – A Rock Star in the Wilderness?

by JAMES HENDRY

I always wanted to be a rock star. Being the focus of ten thousand people in a stadium spectacular always seemed the best possible career. A born performer, I believed I was cut out for a life of glitz and stardom, full of screaming, lust-crazed women flinging bits of their clothing at me. Imagine my surprise when I find myself at an interview for a game ranging course in the middle of deepest Maputaland. How I arrived here is a story all on its own, but suffice it to say that my presence is not entirely of my own design. In fact, I do not even know what a game ranger does.

The next evening I find myself sleeping in a drainage line (or dry watercourse) with a group of people I have never met. The rain is pelting down and I am on lookout, peering into the blackest night I have yet seen with the aid of a student budget torch. I am convinced that we are all about to die at the hands of a pride of man-eaters. A lion calls in the distance and I know, I know that he is calling his friends to plan their assault on our camp.

Six weeks later, I think I may quite enjoy living in the bush. With rock stardom on the back burner and my head swollen with new concepts, I am packed off to a reserve in the South African lowveld where I will complete my training.

I arrive during the height of the floods that are devastating large parts of south-eastern Africa in the early part of 2000. The lodge is closed because it is impossible to manoeuvre a Land Rover loaded with guests more than two feet without becoming mired. As I switch off my little red, mud-bespattered Golf at the reception area Anna, the head chef, emerges brandishing a tall glass. It is four o'clock and she is on to her second gin and tonic. She greets me like a long-lost relative just returned from a prolonged solo expedition to the South Pole. I am just recovering from this when the general manager happens on the scene. He is wielding a .458 calibre Winchester Magnum menacingly, so I smile weakly and look at my shoes, hoping not to be shot within my first few minutes on the reserve. Anna hops into my car and directs me to the room which will serve as my quarters for the next two years.

I know from the beginning that fear is the greatest obstacle I face. The remainder – taking game drives, acquiring knowledge of birds, trees, stars, mammals, etc. – is going to be relatively straightforward. I was briefed during the training course that I will have to complete many tasks, one of which is to walk all of the roads of the reserve, un-armed. Yes, I thought it ridiculous too. It's Big Five country.

At the beginning I even feel scared to walk to my room at night. This is not aided by the fact that the torch I have is the same high-quality recycled plastic one I used for night watch on the training course. Voices in my head keep telling me that there are famished lions behind every bush waiting to devour me. The most fearful part is opening my door as I have to turn my back to the night and thus expose myself to the horde of creatures that have been waiting since sunset to pounce on me while I fumble for the door handle.

The training starts off pretty uneventfully, apart from a brief but vi-cious attack from Anna in the kitchen when she catches me stealing crunchies one morning. I spend the first week in the lodge folding sheets, selling curios (masks, spears, books, etc.), fixing Land Rovers (well, tightening the odd nut in the workshop under strict supervision), baking cakes and answering phones ('Good day, you have reached zero one five four two five six four, my name is James, how may I help you?'). In the afternoons I go on game drives and see things I have only ever seen in documentaries: Leopards, African Wild Dogs and enormous herds of buffalo. So far so good, but in the back of my mind the idea of nine days' unarmed walking lingers menacingly.

The lodge reopens in my third week. A large group of South African doctors arrive for a long weekend. Most of them sink their brand new not-meant-for-off-road SUVs in the mud on the way in and thus turn up a little hot under the collar. After tea, the doctors and their families go off on a game drive and the camp is quiet. The clouds are building and it looks like the deluge may begin afresh. I am on standby, which means that I keep a radio with me at all times in case of emergency, and then assist with any problems that may occur. Quite what the powers that be think I am going to be able to achieve in case of catastrophe I cannot imagine. At this stage I can barely find my own room, let alone begin to fathom the reserve road network.

The rain duly starts at six in the afternoon. By seven o'clock it has not abated and I am just thinking how lucky I am not to be out there on the game drive when the radio crackles to life.

'Standby ranger come in,' says the voice.

'Er, umm, go ahead,' say I, twice – once into the wrong radio orifice and once into the right one.

'The children wish to return home from game drive, please go and fetch them at Mashaba's Rest,' instructs the receptionist on the other end.

Two things about this request worry me. First, it is raining so hard that it is not possible to see more than three feet and I cannot imagine why the children would want to come home and not the adults, surely they are all wet, cold and miserable? Secondly, where in the blazes is Mashaba's Rest?

I don my 'Army & Navy' rain jacket, grab my trusty torch and step out into the storm, discovering very quickly that the previous owner of the jacket had been very poor at ducking enemy shrapnel. I arrive at the workshop to fetch the standby vehicle and ask directions from the mechanics who are celebrating the rain with twenty-four beers each.

I manage to elicit a vague set of slurred directions above the clatter of rain on the tin roof, and then I am off, out into the squall. Up and down the bumps and through the puddles I splash. There is only one road to choose from so I am unable to lose myself just yet. I cross three strongly flowing streams and congratulate myself on being a marvellous exponent of four-by-four driving. When I happen upon the next crossing I have no reason to believe it will be any different from the others. Buoyed by previous success, I plunge into the torrent, but discover quickly that I have grossly underestimated its depth and strength. Water surges up over my lap, the wheels lose traction and the Land Rover starts to float downstream. Miraculously a tyre finds purchase on a rock and the vehicle pulls out to the other side. I am just beginning to marvel at my own magnificence when there is loud scraping crash and the right front wheel disappears into a hole. It has been cunningly disguised by the water streaming down the road. First gear, reverse, wheels left, wheels right. I try everything, but I am going nowhere. What now?

The rain is more enthusiastic than ever now and there is no roof over the game viewer. I try my hand-held radio. It is useless after my river crossing. The vehicle radio works however.

'Reception come in.'

'Go ahead,' says the irritatingly cheerful voice on the other end.

'I am stuck on main road and you need to send the tractor to come and pull me out, I am trying to fetch the doctors' children.'

'OK,' he says, 'what is your position?'

'I am . . .' And with that the radio dies.

It is at this point that the realisation of my predicament sinks in. I am in the dark, in the rain, at night, in the bush where all the nasties live. I determine that the tractor must find me eventually as I am on the only route out of the camp. Little do I know that the river in front of the camp has risen to such an extent that the tractor cannot ford it. I fashion myself a little roof from the blankets in the car and wait.

Fifteen minutes later my roof is leaking as badly as my jacket. I realise I am going to have to extricate myself. I am going to have to get out of the vehicle to retrieve the High Lift jack attached to the rear of the seat frame. But – I am too frightened to climb out. Never mind, I will simply climb over the seats and wrest the jack from the frame by leaning over the back. Over I go and end upside down, legs flailing, as I try to lift the heavy jack over the back seat. Somehow I manage not to fall out into the water behind. This is all highly illogical, of course, as I will have to stand outside the vehicle in order to use the jack . . .

Having conquered my fear of stepping outside the vehicle the hard

34

way I shove the jack into the jacking point and pump the action, all the while checking behind me for the starved creatures of the night. Eventually the front differential clears the ground and I climb back into the driver's seat feeling most relieved to be unscathed. The engine turns over, splutters once and then fires. I ram it into gear and fly forward off the jack and out of the hole. My confidence is returning. I reverse, being careful to avoid the hole, and perform a remarkable feat of athleticism by retrieving the jack without alighting from the driver's seat. I pitch the helpful tool behind me and speed off.

With the aid of my cheap, yet seemingly indestructible, torch I find where I am supposed to be going. Mashaba's Rest is a rustic old bush camp slowly rotting back into the bush. The structure is centred around a large fireplace and outside sitting area. At one end there is a small, roofed deck which affords a superb three hundred and sixty degree view, and below this a sheltered level. At the other end there is a room full of eight seasons' worth of dry mopane leaves, which I am told used to be the loo. The only remaining furniture consists of two iron chairs that are the most uncomfortable things I have ever had the displeasure of sitting in. There are also five rangers, five trackers and thirty sodden and unhappy family members. The kids, who I am supposed to be rescuing, are sleeping in the loft and the adults are trying to doze underneath. Their ability to rest is being hampered by the palls of smoke billowing from a wet wood fire that has been built by the trackers. The rangers cannot believe I have made it there alive and do not know who sent for me. They had, in fact, turned around at the drainage line that nearly took me away. The rest of the evening is spent shifting amongst the puddles, coughing and spluttering, while trying to avoid having to sit in the chairs.

After the rain and jack incident I feel a little braver about the wilderness into which I have been thrust. But, the day before my unarmed walking programme is to begin, five young lions are spotted on the airstrip. In the middle of the day, Chris, the head ranger, decides it would be a good idea if I see them on foot before he sends me out into the wilds all alone and unarmed. What a great idea, I think. Oh what's that? You want me to carry the rifle. In other words you want me to defend you, and the other three, from an attack that will probably come so fast that I won't even have time to soil myself, let alone raise the rifle, chamber a round, take aim and then fire it accurately.

'Right,' I say.

Thankfully Elvis, senior tracker, will be coming along too. He has eyes sharper than the Hubble Telescope and weighs about one hundred and twenty kilograms, so I can hide behind him when the lions attack.

We begin tracking the young males into the thickest mopane I have ever encountered. My heart is about to overtake my lunch in a race to escape my throat. Five minutes later, Elvis stops dead and points.

'Lions,' he says, as though pointing out a dull museum piece.

I look into the bush and see nothing.

'They run,' he grunts with disdain.

Yes, I know they can run. They run really fast! Where are they running and when do I start shooting?

We track them again for a couple of minutes and catch one more glimpse of all five of them fleeing: the king of beasts in full flight at the sight of us. Come to think of it, it is probably Elvis they are scared of; I know I would be.

This is my first real indication that the wild animals out here are not just gleefully waiting to maul me for the sake of it. I do not feel confident but I do feel better prepared for tomorrow.

DAY ONE

I will start at lunchtime today, but am feeling a little green and unable to eat. I am handed a map and set of specific route instructions. Andrew, another ranger, bequeaths me the stick he used on his walks and makes me feel better when he confesses that he was also terrified. Thanks Andrew. I will bash the charging animals to death with a stick. Just before departure I pack a radio, a first-aid kit, a tin of condensed milk, a litre of water, my bird book and my binoculars (which I think are relics of Monty's desert campaign) into a small backpack.

At two in the afternoon I am off – just a short walk to start. It is hot, but it feels good to be walking. I am breathing hard and my heart rate escalates the further from the lodge I march. I spend some time sharpening the end of my stick with the goodly sized fishing knife I am carrying (I must point out here that I own a perfectly crafted Zulu stabbing-spear, which I was declined permission to carry). I figure my best chances of defending myself lie in holding the sharpened stick with my left hand and the fishing knife with the other. I will attempt to lance the charging animal with the stick and if this fails I will catch him (or most likely her) with a side-slicing blow to the jugular, making sure not to allow my hand to slip down the blade and render my palm a useless and bloodied appetizer.

I find the first sign of an animal after almost an hour. I may have passed many others but I am having trouble not staring at the road in front of me, which is precisely what I am not supposed to be doing. I spot a buffalo track and freeze. Taking stock of my predicament I peer into the bush on either side of me. The wind is good and I cannot smell any buffalo. Satisfied that I am not about to be run over, I crouch down to investigate the track more carefully. It has been made in the mud and it has not rained for a week. Never mind, at least I saw it.

The rest of the afternoon yields precious little, I have no hint of any

further encounters with large game or even the adrenaline rush of finding the evidence they have left behind. So, at the end of the day, I have made it back to the lodge alive, with just a small bruise on my thigh where I fell from a marula tree I was trying to climb. I feel satisfied but anxious about the next eight days.

DAY TWO

It is raining and I cannot hear anything for most of walk. It is the last of the relatively short walks and whatever tracks there were have been washed away. Beasts that may have been lurking just off the road are masked by the thick mopane, or the noise of the weather.

DAY THREE

Day three is the first of the longer walks. It is raining again in the morning and I set off wearing my jacket, which makes a racket like the scrunching of a hundred plastic bags. It comes off, so that I may at least hear the charging elephant before it hits me. I am walking through thick mopane woodland, carrying a couple of large stones for extra defence. I am scanning more widely which makes me feel positive. Suddenly there is a scuffling in the long, wet grass in front of me. I skid to a halt and search for the cause of the noise. A hyaena stands up and looks at me. I have not seen hyaenas on foot before so I am not sure how it will react. I am pretty sure it will not see me as a meal, but it shows no sign of moving off. 'Voetsek!' I yell, hurling a stone at the curious-looking carnivore. The stone misses, the hyaena looks hurt, tucks its tail between its legs and hurtles off. I smile to myself and continue. After a while I feel ashamed and resolve not to throw stones at things that do not show any overt desire to have me for breakfast.

A little further on there is an almighty crack. I dive into the bush as the end is surely nigh. Silence. Another crack as a second mopane limb is torn free. It is further away this time. I unravel myself from the foetal position and stand slowly. It can only be an elephant. He has clearly not noticed me – well, to be honest, he is at least a hundred metres away. I head into the woodland south of the road to skirt the unsuspecting pachyderm. I tread as carefully as possible, my stare fixed on where I think the elephant is. I do not hear him again and re-emerge onto the road at a junction where I puff my chest out, feeling quite proud. My only problem is that the sun is hidden behind a thick blanket of cloud. My instructions tell me to head west but I have no idea which of the four roads around me heads west. Five kilometres later I figure out that what I thought was west was in fact south. The day ends with me soggy, safe and slightly less terrified.

DAY FOUR

The weather clears to a fine muggy swelter for the first of the twenty-five kilometre walks. I have prepared for this. In addition to my can of condensed milk, I have a mango, an orange, and a cheese and marmalade sandwich. I am still only carrying one litre of water. A soldier I once met told me that all I need to sustain myself is a stone to suck. He was in some sort of 'special forces' unit and probably crossed the Sahara riddled with bullet wounds so I decide to see if his method works.

My lunch break is at a waterhole and is the highlight of my day; alone in the quiet peace of the March midday. A lone wildebeest bull wanders down to the water's edge. He does not see me in the shade. I feel at ease for the first time.

Quite near the end of the walk I make the fatal error of foot-watching because fatigue and dehydration are setting in. I realise this and look up. I do not know why I look up when I do but there, standing watching me, is the largest elephant I have ever seen. He may in fact be a small one, but the shock factor amplifies his stature. I stop, swear violently and scuttle back behind a tree. He watches for a while and then ambles off. Not so bad, I think to myself.

DAY FIVE

The trackers laugh heartily at me when I tell them where I am walking today. 'Big Bend? No rifle? You mad, Chris mad,' says Jon, who spends most of his days tracking lions unarmed. Great.

Most of the route is along the banks of the seasonal Timbavati River.

In other words the bush is so thick on either side of the road that it makes the Bwindi Impenetrable Forest* look like a fairway. The only consolation is that the innumerable vicious buffalo will probably trip on something as they hurtle out to finish me off. I am walking very, very slowly, listening to every sound. The road smells like a dairy from all the buffalo activity. Halfway through the walk I am supposed to cross the river, but the grass is so tall and thick that I cannot find the crossing. I reason that I will simply have to pick a spot and head across. There is just a trickle in the riverbed at the moment so it should be fine. I hack and crawl my way though the bush to the bank where I carefully check left, right and then jump. It is at this moment that I learn the valuable lesson of looking down before jumping. I land in the sand and look up. Not ten metres away is an ancient buffalo bull. Time stops. We look at each other and consider our options. From my point of view, there in front of me is the animal that any big-game hunter will tell you is by far the most dangerous animal alive. Time begins again. We both explode in opposite directions. He disappears, snorting up the bank and I dive behind a Wild Date Palm thicket and try to breathe.

DAY SIX

It is hotter today than any of the previous days. I am still not sure how to process the experience of yesterday. Should I really be here? Do I need to subject myself to this sort of fear? Did all the other rangers feel this when they walked? Probably not exactly the same, perhaps some were afraid like me, but all would have had to deal with different issues concerning why they had chosen this line of work. I know I will complete the walking programme, I am too stubborn to drop out now, but I am not convinced I will continue this vocation when I have finished. This is a day for contemplation. Much of it is along the riverbank again but the bush is not as thick as yesterday. I am considering all these things and not focusing on the task at hand, which is when it becomes dangerous, so I climb a tree and think about myself, what I am doing and why I am doing it. I cannot come up with the answers,

* A dense tropical forest in Uganda. The home of the Mountain Gorilla.

but I remember that I have always enjoyed being in a beautiful place where I can see the sun set over mountains at the end of the day. I draw peace and meaning from this. Twenty minutes later I continue with methodical determination.

DAY SEVEN

It has been pouring during the night and the Timbavati River is in full flood. I am staying at a bush camp south of the river for the next two nights so that I can walk the south of the reserve. The camp is managed by the hugest man I have ever seen. His name is Bees (pronounced 'beers' and literally meaning 'steer'). All Bees wears is a pair of rugby shorts that would have been too small for me fifteen years ago. His vocabulary consists of obscenities from at least three languages and he uses these liberally to address me and all of his adoring staff.

He sends me on my way in the morning. It is stiflingly hot but I feel good after yesterday's contemplations. The terrain is more open today, which makes for easier awareness. This walk is thirty kilometres long. At the twenty-kilometre point I am walking past a small mopane thicket in the far south of the reserve when I hear a bark. I stop to listen. A moment later twelve African Wild Dogs trot out onto the road thirty metres in front of me. They stop and stare. I am not sure what their reaction will be. Two of the beautiful hounds take a couple of steps towards me.

'Voetsek!' I say with confidence and then immediately regret it.

The dogs dash off to continue their hunting. I am sorry not to have taken the opportunity to spend some more time with them. I continue on in the midday roast, striving to keep my eyes from raking the ground in front of my feet. This approach pays off as an elephant meanders into view a hundred metres down the track. There have been reports of a rogue elephant in the area, alleged to have terrified the wits out of tourists and Kruger National Park staff alike, stomping on cars and bicycles and being generally disagreeable. The calm I have been feeling is overcome by the thought that this must be the recalcitrant bull and that he probably has super senses that will be able to detect me even at a hundred metres. I leap behind a thicket and wait until I am sure he has had

enough time to make it halfway to Cape Town. I jog the rest of the way back and arrive dehydrated but happy in the knowledge that there is only one more solo walk to go.

DAY EIGHT

This is supposed to be my final walk but the river is impassable so I spend the day in camp reading and laughing at Bees as he thunders around the camp in his little blue boxer shorts hurling abuse at buildings, tools, staff and guests.

DAY NINE

My final walk. Before I can walk anywhere I must ford the river.

'Just walk in, you will make it straight across,' says Bees, as we stand surveying the torrent.

Yes Bees, someone of your size would probably be able to move upstream against the Nile in flood. He gives me a shove and I find myself floating rapidly towards Mozambique with my bag held above my head. I reach the opposite bank some way from my target and turn to see Bees rolling about. So begins the long wet trudge home. I see no sign of big game the whole day which is just fine by me.

This is the day to consider what I have learnt from my lone travels. I have learnt a bit about our species' place in the world, something about animals and rather a lot about me. I have realised that despite my obvious physical inadequacy compared with all of the animals around me, they are more fearful of me than I had ever imagined. I remember that my ancestors ambushed, stalked, stabbed, trapped and hounded the animals of Africa. I may have forgotten but the animals remember and they remember well. It is because of this that I am able to walk on this ancient land in careful confidence. If I respect the animals and if I do not threaten them they will leave me alone. In most cases they will flee from me with a haste that defies logic. Impala, zebra, wildebeest, warthog and even diminutive steenbok alarm call and hurtle away when their flight line is crossed.

Even buffalo bulls will just watch me walk by if they perceive no threat. Leopards will quietly sink into the grass unobserved, not to stalk but to hide as I pass. An elephant bull may turn to face me, his ears wide out, throwing dust in the air menacingly, but should I retreat, he will most likely not follow. It is not menace behind his eyes. His aggression is a manifestation of fear, not malice.

I have learnt that there is no such thing as a wantonly aggressive animal. An animal is only dangerous if it is threatened to the point that it sees no option but to defend itself by attack. The trick is to know what will cause an animal to feel threatened like this and for the most part I need only put myself in the animal's position to figure that one out. I need only to face myself with mankind, the most awesome predator the world has ever seen, to know how threatened I would feel.

When I arrive home I expect a large welcoming committee clapping, flinging streamers and patting my back. I anticipate being heralded a fearless warrior who has completed a task few would dare and even fewer would survive. I receive a cursory 'well done' from one or two people. The rest hardly notice. No fanfare? No adulation? I am a bit taken aback by this until I realise that most of the staff have actually been walking in the bush unarmed since childhood and what I have just completed is really just what they have done all their lives.

Super-spectral Vision

It is remarkable how some raptors are able to locate their rodent prey in long grass. Their eyesight is very good, no doubt, but how do they know where to look for that tiny mouse or gerbil from their place on the wind, high above the ground?

A study of kestrels in Finland revealed that they are able to detect fresh rodent runways. The ability to distinguish between old and fresh runways must take more than good eyesight.

Some raptors can probably see into the ultraviolet part of the light spectrum. Although impressive, this ability is by no means unique. There are many animals, birds and insects that have visual capabilities different from our own and that can see wavelengths of light which we cannot perceive. However, some rodents are known to urinate at frequent intervals along their runways and, interestingly, their urine reflects ultraviolet light!

David Hood

Girls Just Wanna Have Fun

(The Making of a Girl Ranger)

by MEGAN EMMETT

'Girls can't be game rangers . . .' was the familiar chant that came from the lips of my exasperated mother every time the subject came up (and it came up regularly, ever since, at ten years old, I had first entertained the notion that a ranger was indeed what I wanted to be when I grew up).

Somehow I never let these remarks deter me and, by the time I finished school, things in South Africa had changed dramatically. Taking full advantage of the new opportunities open to me I decided to study nature conservation.

Nothing in my all-girls-school education, or learnt on casual family holidays to the local game reserve or watching wildlife documentaries on television, did anything to prepare me for the realities and, yes, adventures, of becoming a ranger. Although people of all descriptions had cautioned me, casting dubious looks over my flimsy frame, it wasn't until my first year of technikon, and associated in-the-field training, that the full implication of my chosen career started to dawn on me.

I can't remember if this dawning came the first time the head of department casually spat a list of Latin names at me in passing conversation, or if it was arriving mid-winter at a game reserve only to be told my first official game-ranging task was to sort through barrels of frozen elephant guts – those of a rogue pachyderm dispatched during his attempt to take out a tourist and now destined for the vulture restaurant. Perhaps it was the horror of being transported in a bakkie, during the drive across a roadless stretch of Kalahari, which caught alight every five minutes thanks to an unavoidable accumulation of long grass caught in the protective plates under the vehicle and heated by the exhaust. The message was clear – this was not an easy job!

It's a common misconception that 'game ranging', 'field guiding' or 'bushwhacking', (call it what you like) is in fact glamorous, a real life version of the exciting adventure programmes we see on reality TV, with big bush vehicles, heavy rifles and wild animals. No-one talks about the boring bits or the hours of hard slog maintaining the engines of said vehicles with limited spares (you're in the bush, after all), or the hours spent on the ground tracking the animals – often unsuccessfully. The reality is that ranging – be it in the form of managing a reserve or guiding tourists – is really more like farming than *Survivor*.

It took me years to build my own illusions and I, like so many others, had to learn the reality first-hand. To clarify, let me rewind. As a little girl, I had been precocious at the best of times. For example, taken on holiday to the coast by my family, I was wrestled from my bed early the first morning to walk on the beach with my grandmother. The sun was not quite up and it happened to be a gusty, chilly morning. Determined to enjoy an early morning walk with her grandchild on the beach, despite the miserable weather, my gran encouraged me to put on a tracksuit over my swimming costume. Obediently I did so, thrilled to finally be going to 'see-the-sea'. It wasn't long before we arrived at the windy seaside and I began immediately to remove my warm attire, delightedly exposing my five-year-old potbelly to the freezing elements. Turning around at this point my grandmother shrieked: 'What are you doing child? You'll freeze!' To which I responded, as if it should have been obvious, 'Nanny, you have to look pretty on the beach.'

Like the notion of the bikini being a prerequisite for a beach visitation, the television also impressed, on my young mind, the idea that being in the bush with the wildlife I loved so much was synonymous with the 'rugged bushwhacker' (complete, of course, with Jeep Wrangler!). Reality began to bite when the same 'I must look pretty on the beach' girl was shuffled into ME Stores by her mother, on a mission to kit her seventeen-year-old out for Conservation College. Gracious as she was about my choice of career, an all-knowing motherly 'I told you so' look came into her eyes when I expressed my utter horror at what I saw reflected back at me in the mirror. The stiffly starched, over-sized, made-for-men khakis could hardly be called stylish. It was almost all over in that second. Real doubts flooded my mind for the first time in all my life. Was I doing the right thing? Maybe this wasn't for girls? Self-respecting, fashion-conscious, 'got to fit in at all costs', teen-age ones anyway. Sensing my hesitation (and knowing my passions), my mom assured me that everyone would look the same in the field and that this was, in fact, what was expected of me.

Later I would find out that the ranger is responsible for a great deal of unwarranted attention from complete strangers – known in the industry as 'Khaki Fever'. I dug my heels in as I'd have to do many, many more times on the journey to becoming a *girl*-ranger and left the store *dressed to kill*.

Naturally Mom was right and pretty soon khakis and emerging 'conservationist' were inseparable. Khakis are wonderful. They are cool in summer, warm in winter and they eliminate the 'what shall I wear to-day' syndrome. They can also be useful for wiping grubby hands – like that first day on the job, when my hands were in a mess of elephant guts, or soon after when my student colleagues and I were 'bush-clearing' and they were covered in diesel and Tordon (a chemical used to poison tree stumps). A resultant pong does however accumulate. In mid-winter, there simply is no choice but to put that stinking jacket back on each morning. There's no time between late-to-bed and early-to-rise that accommodates a washing process and even if there was, in freezing conditions, there's no chance the jacket would be dry in time. Nor is there really need for clean kit daily anyway – it only stays that way momentarily. The smell is sometimes compounded by the gore that has accumulated in the back of the Land Rover; the stench in the back of the vehicle (the designated student zone) can be enough to turn the strongest of stomachs . . . for the first few days at least.

This is especially true if that's where you are all night executing such time-consuming tasks as waiting for drugged lions to recover consciousness.

Many wild animals in Africa are endangered to some degree by virtue of the fact that their natural habitat outside of reserves is continuously eroded by human expansion and agriculture. Often, quite intense management is required to simulate appropriate ecological conditions within a reserve limited by unnatural boundaries such as fences, urban areas or physical conflict with man. Paradoxical as it may sound, lions in a finite space, for example, breed well and breed quickly. To minimise interbreeding they sometimes need to be translocated, or exchanged with unrelated individuals. Key animals are thus collared with radio transmitters. The position of the animals can then be monitored at any time. A 'lion call-up' involves a dead impala, disembowelled and dragged behind the already-strong-smelling vehicle in the vicinity of the lions (read: 'blood-covered khakis'), a loudspeaker blaring hyaena 'woops' to attract feline attention and one student to tie the misshapen impala (despite lions in hot pursuit) to a tree. Once this is achieved, the animals can be monitored while they feed, checked for condition or darted for collaring, treatment or removal. The problem thereafter is that the anaesthetic drug, Zoletil, takes a long time to wear off. While the lion recovers it needs to be watched by its human guardians to ward off attack from contending lions or from creatures like elephants that will chase lions as a form of predator deterrence. Apparently these intelligent mammoths, like enemy lions, like to take on their opponents while they are down. Sometimes the only way to deter a herd from trampling a drugged lioness is to drive between the cat and the herd, shifting the vehicle's position as the elephants approach.

Sometimes resident male lions would surround a boma in which a new lion lay recovering, bellowing out their dominance and hostile intent. Nights like that, freezing on the back of the Land Rover in below-zero conditions, hungry, because there had not been time enough to eat before embarking on the task of tracking, calling and darting the lions, and tired, from a twenty-hour work day, reinforced the familiar theme developing in my brain, that this indeed was not easy nor glamorous by any stretch of the imagination. But what it was, what it is, is exhilarating. Even shivering does not diminish the wonder of the stars on a clear winter's night, as you while away the hours. Words cannot adequately describe the terror and absolute awe of lions' powerful roars reverberating about your ears, shuddering the vehicle (and your chest), their breath sending puffs of hot air from their nostrils, so close to you that it almost warms you.

And that was why I was doing this. Something in me had known it all along. It doesn't matter how many hours are spent in the scorching sun or stolen from night-time slumber. The cuts and gashes from thorns and misplaced saws and pangas don't matter, neither do the aches and pains from unfamiliar physical labour. The very fact that you're in the bush amidst innumerable amazing creatures is exhilarating and wonderful and, in fact, addictive. All the effort is watered down by the utter euphoria of being there, in the wilderness, battered by the elements – hot when it's hot, wet when it rains, windswept when the wind blows. A fifteen-minute rest in the shade of a spreading marula is like a blissful holiday at the sea! The sounds are clearer and more poignant, the smell of the bush, the smell of your own sweat, it's a sweetness in your soul.

Small things matter so much it's almost a delirium. Like stumbling upon a prickly pear with ripe fruit after hours in the February sun searching out the parameters of a tide of Triffid Weed (a vicious invader from Cuba that is swallowing the biodiversity in large areas of South Africa). Prickly pears are also invasive alien plants, but the elation of our find and the chance for refreshment caused us to forget to input its location. Nothing ever tastes as good as the fruit of a White Berry Bush picked when there's nothing else to eat and you're stranded in a dry riverbed because a herd of buffalo has surrounded you and inadvertently separated you from your transport while *you're* trying to sneak

up on *them*. A swim never feels as good as when it's in the horse-trough and you're in it in your clothes because there was simply no better option after an 8-hour anti-poaching patrol than to roll from the horse's back into the water. Nothing feels as brilliant as finding that rhino after hours of tracking and neither it, nor its young calf, is aware of your beady eyes studying it from shadows of an *Acacia* tree. The walk back is never as long. I remember feeling more alive than ever the first time I guided a safari with paying international guests. The motherly warnings and earlier bush experiences had prepared me well for this leg of my career and its associated training involving walking 250km of road network, writing 8-hour examinations and more than a visit or two to the shooting range to take on a charging buffalo on wheels. Once I was finally let loose in the 'Big Green' with real guests, I suddenly found myself following a leopard and two cubs through grass so tall it covered the bonnet of the vehicle as we seemingly floated along behind them. Although initially scary (the bush at coal face with others' lives in your hands is a big deal) the satisfaction of being responsible for generating such rewarding experiences was enormous.

Being a woman guide elicits all kinds of reactions from people. Some find it completely fascinating that women rangers can make the Land Rover move in a forward direction without it stammering and stalling, let alone actually locate animals and still find the lodge after four hours of apparently ambling around in random directions. Others find it unbelievable that we can operate a .375 rifle and although you'd assume people would be discreet about their reservations, they seldom are. One burly man sitting directly behind my seat was obviously extremely nervous about leaving the parking lot and taking on untamed Africa with a girl driver. He tapped me on the shoulder while we were still in the parking lot and insisted that I ensure the diff was locked before we departed, giving no thought whatsoever to the fact that I rather than he knew where we were going and exactly what the roads looked like there.

I love what I do, despite the fact that the journey has been tough and continues to be so. I wouldn't change anything for the world – it challenges me constantly. My folks have had small glimpses of my passage to rangerdom and my mom has slowly changed her tune from 'Girls can't be rangers . . .' to a dreamy-eyed, 'If only I could have done this when I was your age.'

Nocturnal Vision

Eyes that reflect in the torchlight at night are eerie. The really spooky thing about them is that they see so much more than we do.

Our eyes, and the eyes of most birds (including owls), don't reflect brightly like antelope or carnivore eyes do. Those animals have a well-developed *tapetum lucidum*, a pigmented layer beneath the retina, at the back of the eyeball, that reflects light. The purpose of this layer is to reflect light straight back through the layer of light-receptive cells in the retina, thereby increasing the stimulus they receive. The light passes through the same cells twice, making their reaction stronger and passing on a clearer image to the brain.

That is not the only way in which nocturnal animals can enhance their sight under low-light conditions. Many of these animals have far more rods than cones in their eyes – the rods are the light-receptive pigment cells that pick up monochrome (colourless) shades, whereas the cones differentiate between various wavelengths of light, therefore picking up colours. The rods are, however, more receptive to light and so having more rods enables them to see better under low-light conditions. This does compromise their colour vision, but seeing colour is not necessarily of much benefit to these animals.

Colour vision is important for some species, such as primates and the many bird species which feed on fruit. Fruit changes colour when it is ripe to signal to these creatures that it is now edible. They eat the juicy fruit and return the favour by helping to disperse the seeds.

It is all a compromise and consequently most birds and

primates lack good nocturnal vision and have to find a safe place to roost before it gets dark. This is why diurnal birds go quiet towards dusk and baboons and monkeys, if they are not already in the trees, hang around near cliffs or tall trees as darkness begins to settle.

Owls are one of the few avian exceptions to the general rule. Whereas most birds probably have nocturnal vision far inferior even to our own, owls can see better than humans can. While this may seem obvious, their vision is perhaps not quite as good as we would expect: they have a visual capability that is a little better than twice our own, significantly inferior to that of nocturnal mammalian carnivores such as cats, which may see up to eight times better than us at night. However, owls can see colour and this no doubt limits their nocturnal vision somewhat. They cannot see infrared radiation, and probably rely heavily on hearing to detect their prey. Owls have a remarkable ability to judge both distance and direction precisely by hearing alone. Special feathers around the ear holes and facial disc and the asymmetrically positioned ears of some species probably contribute to this ability.

David Hood

Tracker

(In the Footsteps of South Africa)

by JAMES HENDRY

The tracker is a vital component of any game drive experience. The ideal tracker has an almost mystical invincibility about him. I have been fortunate to work with many trackers during my time as a guide, some good and some who should perhaps have been engaged in other professions. They have all instructed me on aspects of the natural world that are not to be found in textbooks. This is a story about good trackers and one particularly excellent tracker whom I had the singular pleasure of working with for a number of years.

The tracker's job is to spot animals and their signs from the front of the vehicle. He must assess the age of the tracks and, if they are fresh enough, it is his responsibility to coordinate the task of finding the animal in question. A good tracker will spend most of his time looking for tracks and signs, but he will not be limited to big game; he will point out birds, flowers and even insects if that is what his guests enjoy. He will hop off the vehicle at any available opportunity to follow fresh tracks, thriving on the challenge and thrill of discovery. A poor tracker assumes the role of 'hood ornament'. He presupposes that visitors to Africa only want to see the Big Five and will wheeze and sigh when the guide stops to look at birds, small antelope or, worst of all, trees.

One of a tracker's most crucial functions is to impart his vast bush knowledge to a wet-behind-the-ears guide with a big ego, loads of theoretical information and very little practical experience. Just about all trackers have grown up in and around wild areas and therefore have a more natural aptitude and understanding of environmental interactions. To this end, the relationship that develops between tracker and guide is paramount. A game drive is enriched immeasurably by a respectful and dynamic relationship between guide and tracker. They will exchange ideas on animal behaviour, tracking and birding. The guide learns huge amounts from being on foot with his tracker. They track and view big game on foot at close quarters and should they have to stand down a charge they must trust each other's courage. More importantly they have the opportunity to learn about their respective backgrounds and hopefully rediscover the world through each other's eyes.

Most of the trackers in the lowveld are either Shangane people who grew up in the area or one-time refugees from Mozambique who have walked barefoot across the Kruger National Park in search of work. For many the tracking trade was learnt early on. As young boys it was their responsibility to herd the family's cattle to community grazing lands before school. After school the cattle had to be retrieved and the easiest way to achieve this was to follow their tracks. Thus tracking was ingrained from childhood. Many people in the rural areas surrounding the Kruger National Park are unemployed and thus poaching (less now than before) is sometimes the only means of obtaining protein. Tracking becomes an important means of survival for some.

I believe one of the reasons that rural South Africans pick up the art of tracking so much more quickly than city folk lies in the fact that they seem to have a better visual perspective of the world around them. Indeed, trainee rangers from farming backgrounds often have a distinct advantage over their town dwelling counterparts. People with rural backgrounds generally have a better three-dimensional perception of the world and an eye for details such as a small indent in the soil, a tiny scuff on a sapling or recently grazed grass. The reason for this may lie in the fact that most of us from urban backgrounds spend our formative years sitting with our heads in books or our eyes glued to the TV. In fact from a young age we spend enormous amounts of time with our eyes focused on words and images less than a metre from us, while our rural contemporaries are scanning the horizon and scouring the ground for telltale signs of dad's cattle.

Few trackers have any formal training whatsoever. Some spend years doing other jobs such as waiting tables before attempting tracking and then prove spectacularly successful at it. Others never do anything else. What definitive qualities make an excellent tracker? There are many things: An eye for detail, eyes that have a superb ability to perceive depth and colour, an understanding of animal behaviour, local knowledge of an area, a 'sixth sense' for predicting animal movements and presence. To go with these, an ability to patiently concentrate for long periods is paramount. It is probably this characteristic more than any other that separates an excellent tracker from a good one. Tracking can be a frustratingly slow process and many of the best eyes in the business quickly become bored and frustrated while slightly inferior peepers succeed in tracking down their quarry because the mind behind them is meticulous, patient, stubborn and focused.

When I began my career as a guide I was awed by many of the trackers at the lodge. Being a good tracker carries status – and so it should. Some go for the macho approach. They don large hunting knives on their belts and regale all and sundry with tales of their courage and skill. Normally the superior trackers are easy to spot. They command a quiet respect by virtue of their obvious skill. They talk very little of dangerous situations as they are not proud of them.

I was particularly taken by the head ranger's tracker. His name is Elvis (and, no, he cannot sing, nor does he want to sing, and if you ask him to sing for you he will smile politely as if you are the first person to ask him). Elvis is a giant. He is about six foot five and weighs at least one hundred and twenty kilograms. He is a man of very few words, but when you are as big as Elvis is you do not need to say much to make a point. He has an interesting history that gives some insight into his character.

Elvis was born in Mozambique circa 1970. When he was seventeen he realised that, other than joining one of the warring factions, there was not much for a young man to do in a poor country wracked by ongoing civil conflict. Elvis did not fancy himself as a soldier so he packed up what he had and headed for South Africa illegally. He took with him a friend his age and a woman with her suckling child. This was a risky business for a number of reasons. Wild animals are an obvious danger to someone who has little bush experience and when you are travelling in the night the dangers become more pronounced. Then there was always the chance of being caught by the security police in apartheid South Africa. It took them fully two weeks to arrive on the western boundary of the Kruger National Park. It would probably have taken less time were it not for the drought. Elvis had to keep leaving the group to find water, which he achieved by tracking elephants to their drinking spots.

Once out of the park, he made his way to the mining town of Witbank on the highveld where his uncle lived. He was too young to be employed on the mine where his uncle worked but he managed to learn to speak Zulu and a smattering of English. His home language was a dialect of Shangane very similar to that spoken in the lowveld, but most of the Shangane-speaking South Africans could also speak another of the country's languages such as Sotho or Zulu. A refugee who could speak nothing but Shangane stood the risk of arousing suspicion from the police.

Four months later Elvis tracked down his brothers Jules and January and he moved back to the lowveld to be with them. They convinced him to enrol at a local school as they felt he would have more opportunities with a bit of education. Just before he could write his seventh grade exams, his aging parents arrived from Mozambique and this necessitated his finding employment to support them.

He spent a month fixing roads and picking tomatoes in the Hoedspruit area, but the salary of seventy rand a month convinced him to look elsewhere. Meanwhile Jules, who was working for the Timbavati Private Nature Reserve as a hunting tracker, managed to secure Elvis a place as a labourer where he fixed roads and skinned animals for the hunting operation. In his spare time Jules taught his brother the rudiments of tracking and six months later convinced his employers that Elvis had potential as a tracker, and so began his distinguished career. He worked for the hunting operation for seven years before moving to a private game reserve in 1993; he was still there when I caught up with him in early 2000.

During my training I was sent out regularly with the trackers to search for animals. It was during these times that I became familiar with the many personalities on the concession's tracking team. I was mainly chauffeur and weapon bearer on these excursions as I could not distinguish an impala track from a lion's. One of the things I learnt was that every tracker has a signature technique of shining the spotlight at night. Obed conducted what looked like a celestial ballet, so graceful were the movements of his beam. Norman shook his light up and down with such violence that one can only assume he had delusions of being the lighting technician at a rave club. Sandros's head moved in opposite directions to his spotlight beam (which was a bit confusing). Elvis swung his light from side to side at a speed that resulted in nausea after five minutes of trying to follow it. Some guests used to ask if he was perhaps trying to warn animals we were coming rather than spot them.

One morning I was dispatched to 'help' Elvis and Zub Zub track a leopard. Zub Zub is as small as Elvis is large. He is an irascible character who speaks no discernable language. Tracking a leopard and her two cubs is a potentially explosive experience as a leopardess with cubs is not known to favour the attentions of humans on foot. So it was with caution that we climbed off the Land Rover to follow some fresh tracks. I lugged the rifle about after Elvis and Zub as they scoured the ground for clues.

The two of them peered at the ground, pointing at practically invisible pugmarks and scuffs that I struggled to make out even when they were shown to me. The tracks moved down into a shady drainage line. We split up briefly. Elvis and I looked at the sand on the streambed

while Zub checked the top of the bank. Elvis spotted her tracks. He reasoned that her cubs must have been close as the tracks were to-ing and fro-ing from a sheltered cranny in the next bend. Zub was examining the boughs of a dark Jackalberry for a dappled golden sheen or perhaps the dangling limb of a recently hoisted carcass, when she
exploded out from under his feet. Zub had been tracking for many years and this development apparently did not excite him overly.

'Pasop!¹' he hissed.

Elvis and I turned to see the startled cat come flying down the bank towards us. I flung the rifle to my shoulder while ripping the bolt open and ramming a round home. It must have taken less than a second but there was nothing to aim at. She had disappeared. I forced my heart back down my throat, uncocked the rifle and turned to look at Elvis. He was looking at a bird above his head.

'Hell, that was close!' I panted.

'Ja,' he said, staring at a Little Sparrowhawk.

That was my first real tracking experience with Elvis and I thought he and Zub were either very experienced or very stupid to be that calm about a charging leopard. I also realised that the leopard could easily have mauled us both before I had had time to think about the rifle, let alone load it. She was simply trying to extricate herself from a situation that was threatening to her and her cubs.

Soon afterwards I was on foot with Elvis again. We were tracking rhino this time, which for a tracker of Elvis' calibre is not particularly challenging. He walked as fast as if he had been following a six-lane highway. After ten minutes or so he spotted two huge grey lumps and pointed them out to me. He then handed me the radio and instructed me to

1 Watch out!

call the game drives to look at the rhino we had found. 'You call,' he said, 'I go toilet.' He wandered off, unbuckling his belt as he went.

I had no idea where I was. I could hear a vehicle in a direction that I thought was south so I instructed the ranger to head north. The engine noise started to fade rapidly.

'South, tell on him south!' hissed Elvis, from behind a Guarri bush. This I did and the revving of the engine grew louder. Unfortunately we were surrounded by a concentration of thorn trees. The rhino heard the vehicle smashing trees from a mile off, turned tail and ran. The Land Rover full of guests hove into view just in time to see a large grey bottom disappearing into the thorns at top speed. As a consolation they were treated to the sight of big Elvis emerging from his bush looking relieved and doing up his belt. 'You seen on a rhino?' he enquired.

On another such expedition I was driving the vehicle for Elvis and Norman (also a tracker) when we spotted a leopard on the road. She moved off into a dense thicket. The responsibility for staying with the elusive cat for the other game drives who wanted to see her thus fell to me. Into the bush we headed, smashing stumps and pushing over trees while Elvis and Norman hid under the seats. As the next vehicle arrived I was feeling rather bullish for finding her (well, admittedly, she found us) and then staying with her. Feeling thus buoyed I waved royally to Eric as he drove past me. He smiled and then his face changed as if he had something really urgent to say but no time to say it. The front of my vehicle plunged into a ditch that I had failed to notice. Eric laughed heartily and disappeared after the leopard.

In such situations, the most obvious course of action is to fetch the jack, hoist the vehicle up and then stuff a lot of sticks and rocks under the wheels. I was about to slide out of the driver's seat when Elvis hopped off and walked to the front of the vehicle. 'Yima,[2]' he said, peering under the car.

He then hooked his huge hams under the bull bar, lifted and said, 'Famba![3]' I fumbled for the key, turned it, rammed the gear lever into reverse and dropped the clutch. To my astonishment, the Land Rover lurched out of the hole. Elvis stood in front and dusted himself off as I stared at him open mouthed. 'Nkomu,[4]' said I sheepishly.

'Ja,' said Elvis, with typical verbosity, while Norman sat in the back laughing and sucking on a cigarette.

It was probably at this point that I realised I needed a tracker with Elvis's Job-like patience if I was ever going to make it as a guide. His calm measured approach would be a perfect foil for my unpredictable impracticality. This was what I (and my future guests) needed in order to explore the reserve and remain relatively unscathed. So when he was eventually assigned to me it was a great relief, but I did feel a little sorry for him.

The most immediate concern was learning to communicate with Elvis. I had learnt a smattering of formal Zulu at school and had studied it for a year at tertiary level, so that was the language we settled on. Elvis has a very special way of speaking English that only those who have spent considerable time talking with him understand. He believed that English pronouns were entirely interchangeable. 'We' was his favourite one. He would point out some rhino tracks to me as he hopped off his seat to check if they were worth following. 'Where did they go?' the guests would ask.

'The rhino, we going on there,' he would say, heading off on foot, with which the guests would all alight from the vehicle and try to follow him.

'No, no, no!' I would say, grabbing one or two of the more enthusiastic ones by the collar, 'he meant *he* went in there, not *we*.'

He also used some interesting word agglomerations. Knob Thorn

2 Wait.
3 Go!
4 Thanks.

thicket became 'knobstornstick'. False Marula thicket became 'fox-marulstick'.

Then he might find a leopard on foot, return to the vehicle and when he could see it again he would turn to the guests and say, 'We seen on a leopard?' Of course those of us with normal eyes had no way of discerning one black rosette in the deep shade of Natal Mahogany tree.

I was often dependent on Elvis to help me position the Land Rover safely around a nervous breeding herd of elephants, or to know where to drive so that rhinos would not run away and how to park the vehicle so that our guests could take award-winning photographs with tiny disposable cameras. I was really a hopeless exponent of Land Rover driving. This was not helped by the fact that as the new guy I was given the oldest Land Rover in the fleet. The steering was set up to give you a full upper-body workout while you drove. The front wheels had such a tenuous link to the steering column that the vehicle would careen off-road every time I turned around to explain some piece of ecology to my guests. I changed gears at the wrong times, mistimed bumps and kept driving off the road. One night, while driving home in a howling gale, I was yelling something about chameleon biology to my guests when one of them shouted: 'Snake!'

I slammed the brake and looked forward just in time to see Elvis flying, Superman style, off his seat and over a bush on the side of the road. The snake turned out to be a stick. As Elvis emerged dusting himself off, I waited for a bludgeoning. He reaffixed himself to his seat without uttering a sound. As we continued I said, 'Sorry Elvis.'

'Ja.'

In the days before hand-held radios, trackers had a hard time at our reserve. The most effective way to find game was to do it on foot because the blocks between roads were vast and the bush very thick in many areas. Spotting game was difficult and it was not possible to simply drive and check if tracks crossing into a block came out the other side. The good trackers spent very little time on the front of the vehicle. Instead, if fresh tracks were found, trackers would trail on foot. In order to communicate with their guides, bits and pieces of superfluous clothing were left dotted about the reserve. The items were usually arranged in an arrow, designating the direction of movement. At first perhaps a jersey hung on a tree, then a woolly hat, after the hat a shirt, then a sock and so on until guests were treated to a sighting of a smiling tracker, pointing at the rhino he had just tracked for two hours, dressed in nothing but his boots and underpants.

The trackers who were prepared to apply themselves became the best followers in the business. They learnt the value and discipline of patience and they also learnt the pure joy of tracking and finding an animal on foot and then receiving the well-deserved adulation from guests awed by the exposition of this ancient art.

Elvis spent very little time on his seat. He quickly got bored with pointing out animals. He would find tracks on the road, jump off and tell me to meet him at a point where it seemed the tracks were heading. Normally he was not there when I arrived.

On one such occasion we were driving four guests – a couple and a father-daughter duo, and although the two groups were unrelated, they were perfectly suited. Jennifer and her husband Bill were from Johannesburg and had every piece of camera equipment known to technology. Jennifer was determined to show me the auras that she could see around trees. She was at pains to point out that the Natal Mahogany tree has a very friendly aura but thorn trees do not. Jeff, eight-year-old Nina's dad, was not sure whether it was hip to be seeing auras around trees or not, so he spent most of his safari screwing his eyes up and staring vacantly at all of the trees proclaiming, 'Yes, yes I think I've got this one.'

While he was staring into the ether his daughter was using the Land Rover as a jungle gym.

In the meantime, Elvis had spotted some leopard tracks

on the road ahead, pointed them out to me and informed me of his intentions in fewer words than anyone else would have managed. He then disappeared into the bush.

I arrived at the designated meeting place to find nothing, so I stepped out of the vehicle and scoured the road for leopard tracks. Nothing. Thinking I may have overlooked them I sought Elvis's tracks, which are considerably bigger than leopards'. When I could not find these either, I grinned toothily at my guests and told them to sit tight and walked off roughly in the direction of where I thought Elvis should emerge. Once out of earshot of my eccentric companions, I whistled in vain for ten minutes before returning to the car. Jennifer was animatedly pointing out the friendly aura surrounding a Jackal-berry tree to Jeff. His daughter was trying to play with Bill's camera and he was about to bash her with a six-foot lens when I emerged.

'Where's Elvis?' they all chimed.

'He is tracking,' I mumbled, and then drove off violently before they could ask anything else. Eventually I found his tracks on the road and followed them until an hour later we saw him on the road ahead, his jersey slung over his shoulder in the late morning heat. He had been walking waterless for three hours. As we approached he turned and smiled. 'Any luck?' I enquired.

'I leave the tracks heading east in the block.'

'A bit hot out there.'

He tipped his woolly hat on his head and smiled, 'Ja.'

It was such privilege and, at the same time, a frustration to walk with Elvis because he followed the vaguest signs much faster than I could even see them. I still cannot quite understand how his eyes so quickly discerned the slightest indentations in the ground and the faintest scuff on a hard surface. I never learnt as much as I would have liked from him because most of the time he was trying to find animals for our guests and my inability to fathom his art would have impacted their experience. When we did find animals on foot it was a particular joy, especially if I thought I may have contributed in any small way. Tracking lions in thick bush or running into buffalo bulls lying in thickets can be nervy stuff and although I was ultimately responsible for our safety, Elvis's confidence (not complacency) was infectious. We watched lions brawling over a giraffe carcass from twenty metres without them knowing we were there. We followed leopards through riverine vegetation so dense that we would stop every few steps to listen for a betraying pant or growl. We found ourselves surrounded by a pack of wild dogs, having unwittingly walked into the middle of them as they slept in the afternoon heat.

Most of the time, however, Elvis tracked alone, usually for hours. When he found his quarry he called me on the radio and directed me into the block where he had discovered the animal at the end of its tracks. I would then head into the block as Elvis directed me by the sound of crashing trees and revving. Our guests ducked under branches, holding on to seat frames as the vehicle lurched and bounced over logs and rocks. Often, if it was a rhino we were after, it was moving with the result that Elvis would keep redirecting me and we might spend up to an hour off-road.

We were once driving a group of English visitors, who were rather nervous of being in wildest Africa. Elvis found a rhino miles off the road. I reminded my passengers to hold on tight and watch out for the thorns before plunging off the road. After half an hour of being redirected through deep drainage lines and hectares of impenetrable Flaky Thorn thicket, I decided enough was enough. The temperature gauge was creeping up. I turned to the guests and suggested we try again later. They were all on the floor of the vehicle whimpering quietly and were only too happy to call it quits. Of course I still had to extricate us from the block. The vegetation became progressively thicker and thornier as I endeavoured the extrication. When I eventually caught up with Elvis we were still some way from the road and there was steam billowing from under the bonnet. The guests were dead silent and spent some time removing thorns, grass seeds and twigs. I asked if they would like some tea and I thought they might cry with relief. While I set up the tea table and poured the comforting cuppas, Elvis opened the bonnet to examine the damage. Quite suddenly there was a mighty 'whooosh' as a fountain spurted forth from the radiator. Elvis dived for cover. Soon thereafter my terrified guests, dressed in thorn-ripped rags, were screaming and lunging for shelter as the superheated water cascaded down between them. We returned home rhinoless and in scorched silence.

I always looked forward to our drinks stops in the evening, especially if we were driving people, such as Spaniards, who could not speak English. I have never met a Spanish person who can speak English, but then again I have met very few South Africans who can speak Spanish. Anyway, if this was the case, we would serve them their drinks (we would of course have to guess what they wanted) and then retire round the back of the Land Rover. While they smoked a hundred cigarettes and yelled at each other, Elvis and I would have our own discussions.

I asked him about his history. He told me about his trip across the Kruger National Park, his childhood and how he learnt to track. I was always amazed at how matter-of-fact he was. He never indicated that he felt he had been dealt a rough hand. He simply explained the way it was. He told me about his family, which included eleven brothers, and his blind father, whom he managed to wrest from poverty in Mozambique. It was during these times that I learnt the most from him.

I would look up at the emerging stars and then we would deliberate on the universe from our different perspectives. I tried to explain that the stars were all like the sun but just so far away that it was difficult for us to imagine how far. Then he might ask me if I believed in God because he did not see how anyone could not when faced with the unfathomable complexity he saw above and around him. He had never seen the sea and we talked about it on a number of occasions. He asked if it was bigger than the reserve we worked on and I tried to give him some idea by telling him that it was bigger than the distance to Johannesburg and back. He was utterly astounded when he did eventually come face to face with the Indian Ocean.

So I came to realise that although Elvis had helped me make the correct decisions for my guests and taught me more about animal behaviour than any book, the most valuable lessons he taught me were about himself as a person and also as an extension of rural South Africa. I came to understand that the education gap that exists between the traditional 'haves' and 'have-nots' is vaster than I ever imagined, and that it will take generations to recover. Mostly Elvis showed me that it is possible for a brave heart, free of bitterness, to achieve relative contentment, against the odds, through courage, self-belief and stoic discipline.

Firewood and Elephant Nests

Most of South Africa's 'private game reserves' have a history of colourful owners from a bygone era. This one was once owned by a German bachelor. Elderly and of poor health, he'd moved away from his beloved bush home to the city, bequeathing the land to the greater conservation authority in the area and leaving the care of his homestead to a humble (if not equally aged) local Shangane man. It is not generally the practice on reserves to collect firewood in large volume, but the exception was made for this caretaker who lived alone in the centre of the reserve.

He would scout the area around the homestead and make neat little piles of wood beside the road for easy removal at a later stage. Sometimes these would appear between the morning and the afternoon drives and guests, noticing these sudden appearances on roadsides they had travelled previously, would enquire as to their origin, unaware of an old Shangane eking out an existence amidst the lions and elephants that they have come to see.

On one such occasion, driving past a pile that had grown unusually large, I muttered jokingly to my guests that the pile was in fact an elephant nest. Now I am not in the habit of lying to my guests. I had simply been making a joke, thinking today that it was especially obvious that this was indeed a pile of firewood. Amused with my own comment, I continued driving, looking for real elephants and other game. I was startled to hear the lady behind me comment quite seriously to her husband, 'Wow, I really didn't realise elephants made nests!' and then to me, 'Megan, how many sleep in the nest at once?'

Megan Emmett

Whatever You Do, Don't Run!

(In a Tributary of the Mighty Timbavati, South Africa)

by DAVID HOOD

Kagiso was a big man. The kind of man you felt you could trust. He did not carry a rifle because where he worked, rifles were not allowed. Still, being a local, he inspired a kind of trust. He was at one with the land. He would know what to do.

So when the lion charged, he had it all under control. He really did. He stood his ground and shouted at the lion. The lion responded to his brave efforts. It stopped its charge. It stopped just metres from him.

So Kagiso, who had it all under control, turned to tell the guests what to do next. But when he turned to look behind him, *there were no guests*!

So the story goes.

Years after I heard this story, I found myself working at a small, tented trails camp. It was in a beautiful area and one of the things that stands out about it in my memory is the dappled shade.

At midday when the summer sun beat down the ground was always dappled. The tent roofs were dappled and, before the sun had reached its zenith, the narrow sandy riverbed in front of the camp was dappled too.

There is something so serene about the variegated, dappled shade made by leaves, something deliciously soothing. It is as if the multitude of shapes resonates with the complexity of our souls and gives us a pattern we can trust.

Once or twice, in this camp, I was able to sleep until after sunrise. On these occasions, if I looked through the gauze window of my dome-shaped tent, I could see the sun rising behind the trees and sparkling amongst the gently swaying leaves of a Jackal-berry or bushwillow.

The same sun cast living shadows on the wooden tables, around which we sat for a hearty brunch after our morning walks. It was always pleasant to sit outside and watch the shadows change shape on the ground and on the Magic Guarri bushes around us. With the recent memory of game viewed from our own two feet and the subtle ache of muscles well used, brunch always tasted delicious.

It was the tamboti trees around this outdoor cooking and dining area that generously supplied most of the cooling shade. With straight, dark trunks, cracked like a reptile's scales, they rose up before spreading angular branches to produce a rather untidy crown. Late in autumn, all the leaves turned to bright shades of yellow and red. Then, one by one, they began to fall from the tree.

I was watchful at this time of year because the tamboti is a deceptive tree. Within its trunk, branches and leaves courses a white latex full of deadly toxins. I had accidentally tasted this sap when I absentmindedly bit into a leaf. I realised my mistake quickly but it left my mouth burning for hours and I knew that even a tiny leaf falling unnoticed into a guest's bowl of cornflakes could cause a reaction far more serious than that which I had experienced!

Like the beautiful yet deadly tamboti tree, the wilderness is both a constant source of delusion and a fountain of enlightenment. Together the two enable us to move forward spiritually. One experience at this little trails camp brings to mind the delusory power of nature:

It was early one morning and we were gathered beneath the tamboti trees for a walk. We had had our coffee and had sprayed repellent on our legs in an effort to discourage the tiny pepper ticks that love to feast on our blood. Once we were all prepared, I explained our plans for the morning's expedition. I had with me my ever faithful and dependable tracker, Jonas, and eight guests. Eight guests make a big group and the maximum number that were permitted on a trail. These guests were all South Africans. Having been to other reserves, they were very conscious of the fact that they knew some things. All too aware that a little bit of knowledge is the most dangerous kind, and conscious of the size of the group, I had briefed them carefully on safety before the walk the previous afternoon. I ended my brief with what has become one of the biggest clichés in the eventful world of bush-walking. 'Should we surprise an animal,' I said, 'whatever you do, don't run.' I explained how, should we come across something unexpectedly, everyone should look to me and I would direct them. They were very confident and eager to set out. Unbeknown to them, their confidence, misplaced as it was, was about to be tested in a way they were not prepared for.

We set out from beneath the branches of the tamboti trees and climbed down a steep bank onto the flat sandy riverbed of the 'Tswat-semoso'. Here you could always see rhino tracks and there would often be the flattened ovals left by elephant's feet. Regularly there would be lion tracks here too. It was always rewarding to see the sudden dawn of realisation in guests' eyes. There really *were* lions here, right here! We were walking where they had walked!

And that was it! Centuries of civilization were stripped away in an instant. Everything the human race had ever achieved suddenly meant very little because here we were, walking with the lions – just like the first people had done. We became humble because we were vulnerable. That is the power of nature.

Sometimes people struggle to embrace this power. Sometimes they have just cut themselves off too much, they have compromised their souls in the pursuit of riches. I worried that these guests were like that. Nature, given enough time, will always break through, but for now, my job would be more difficult.

We headed up the opposite bank of the river and waded through tall, dry grass, until we reached a small grove of Silver Cluster-leaf trees. Here I demonstrated to the guests how you could strip the bark from young branches to make an excellent and amazingly strong rope. I cut a smaller branch and showed them how to make a toothbrush from the same tree and explained how Silver Cluster-leafs always grow just above specific areas called seep-lines. Seep-lines can often be seen from the air as narrow winding lines of greener, more open vegetation. The green is a direct result of moisture percolating through the soil and coming to the surface where a permeable substrate meets a less permeable one and forces the liquid to flow sideways rather than downward. Seep-lines generally follow topographical contours and are an important clue when looking for a place to bore for water.

Nearby, high up in an enormous Rain Tree, we looked at a nest built by a raptor specialising in hunting game birds. The African Hawk Eagle is nearly always seen in pairs. Most eagles form very strong pair bonds but you will seldom find the pair of another species together with as much consistency as this hawk eagle. The reason for this appears to lie in their hunting technique. African Hawk Eagles seem to be co-operative killers! They fly fast through the trees or stoop from above to ambush unsuspecting francolin and guineafowl. If the game birds see them in time, they will often flush, taking to the air on a flurry of wings and flying low, perhaps to the nearest thicket. It is then that the aggressor's partner swoops in from another angle. Dodging branches with fine adjustments of partially folded wings, the second hunter closes in at speed. The game bird flaps its broad wings frantically, but it is trapped. It tries to change direction, but the closest hunter rams sharp talons into warm muscle. A few downy feathers drifting earthwards become the only memento to its passing.

We continued our walk, studying plants and looking at birds with our binoculars. I was trying hard to show the guests something of the wonder of nature. On the ground, tracks and bones provided interesting clues to the area's inhabitants and their habits. We saw various animals too, mostly at a distance, but it was on our return a few hours later that we were to have our most spectacular view of a mammal.

We were less than a kilometre from home and were following the same riverbed that ran past the camp. My intention was to follow its course through the thicker surrounding bush back to the place we had entered it.

The white sand of this dry watercourse varied from less than ten metres to nearly thirty metres in width. The banks were well vegetated and, in most places, quite steep. At irregular intervals, well-trodden game trails led up the banks on both sides. The width of the riverbed and the nature of its course generally allowed for good visibility ahead. Most of my attention was therefore focused on the banks where I was hoping we would spot antelope such as Greater Kudu or Bushbuck as well as birds such as firefinches, orioles or helmet-shrikes.

It was on one of these banks that I spotted a big grey lump. I signalled to the multitude of guests behind me that they should stop. No talking was allowed while we were moving, so all was quiet and hand signals were the preferred means of communication.

The grey lump was just over twenty metres from the white sand where we stood. Although it was partly obscured by bushes, its size and wrinkles left us in no doubt that it was an elephant. It was on its side and this fact, due to recent events in the reserve, brought Jonas to his initial conclusion: 'One that they shot.' He whispered close to me.

A terrible thing had taken place a few months earlier in a nearby part of Kruger National Park. Herds of elephant had been trapped between two fires. The only escape was through the flames. Many of the elephant that had survived this ordeal came into our area of the park. I came across them a few times – never an uplifting sight.

The fire had caused surface skin to peel off in large quantities. Layers of grey skin hung like old tattered rags from the victims' bellies and ears. Their lips, trunks and sides were also badly burnt. Some of the unfortunate creatures had massive cracks, more than a centimetre wide in the sides of their feet. Within these cracks, the flesh was black.

They were in considerable pain. I remember watching a young cow, all on her own – cows are very rarely unaccompanied – standing in the shade of a guarri thicket. She was holding one foot up so that only the toes rested on the ground, and she was rocking. She was moving her giant body back and forth and flexing her trunk restlessly. Her eyes were open and she just kept rocking. Then she'd move to another position and keep rocking.

It seemed, for all the world, that she was willing something to go away. It was impossible to tell, but I wondered whether that something was the pain in her skin and feet or the memory of the death and distress she had witnessed.

For days the helicopter flew back and forth, looking for injured elephants that could be treated. The patients would be darted, smeared with salve and then left to continue their devastated lives. It was all that could be done, the burns would take time to heal and the elephants would have to search for whatever remained of their herds. Those that were too badly injured were shot. Thirteen elephant were shot in our area.

I listened to my tracker's hushed words and nodded. It was the most likely explanation, but I kept looking at the elephant. Something was not right. As I watched, the side of the elephant's massive chest rose slightly and then fell again.

'It's sleeping,' I whispered to my companion and signalled for him to lead on.

We were exactly opposite the grey shape, so either direction would have been a retreat. I decided to continue towards the camp. In a situation like this, it is the ranger's duty to remain between the guests and the animal – which may potentially become a threat. My tracker knew this and was well trained as to his duties in such a situation. The guests had been briefed too that when moving away from a big animal, they were to follow the tracker and I would bring up the rear.

Keeping an eye on the sleeping form, Jonas began to lead on down the riverbed. I, meanwhile, signalled the guests to follow his lead. There was no way I could whisper loudly enough to explain the situation fully to all eight guests. It was for instances like this that we briefed guests on safety before going walking. Because we had stopped, they could see we were looking at something, but all I could do was whisper to the first few guests that there was a sleeping elephant and that they should follow my tracker immediately. To the rest I signalled for them to keep coming, hoping to be able to whisper an explanation to the others as they passed. Some of the guests were reticent and responded more slowly to my hand signals than the situation demanded. They had seen the elephant now and thought they had it under control. They had no idea.

Most of the group had passed behind me when the elephant stood up. The quiet lump of grey was instantly transformed into a towering tusker. I watched as he took a few steps in our direction. He was up on a bank, nearly two metres above the riverbed and, with his big ears spread, he was coming closer. He had been woken unexpectedly, perhaps he had smelled us, and his initial reaction seemed to be to investigate the disturbance. He looked really big from this angle. He was an awesome sight, but out of the corner of my eye I could see something else. My brave guests were running for their lives! In that moment their confidence had vanished.

There was no easy way up the opposite bank and my tracker managed to stop their desperate flight further down the riverbed. Sensibly, he had kept walking quickly away from the elephant.

The elephant stopped after a few steps and was no more than twenty metres from where I stood. I continued down the riverbed to catch up with the guests, wary also that the elephant's curiosity might change into something else. With guests, extra caution is always called for. My tracker was well ahead of me and the group was spread out.

Then, as I approached, two of the men at the back of the group stopped to look at the elephant. They stood, suddenly defiant of the great beast. I had no time for this show of false bravado. 'Keep moving!' I ordered as I marched towards them. I was incredulous.

The elephant watched us go and I could feel a sense of achievement amongst my guests. I did not feel the same, I did not believe there was achievement here, we had not fought, we had not stood our ground against a worthy adversary. We had woken an old man and for that we should be ashamed.

Half an hour later, we were sitting in the shade of the tamboti trees.

It was a familiar and therefore comforting setting. I realised that I didn't much like these guests. In fact, I really disliked their arrogance. Of course, that was irrelevant, I had to get on with them. I found myself begrudging the fact that they had had such a close encounter with such a special creature.

Yet, who was I to judge them? What right did I have to decide which of God's creations was more special than another?

The sleepy elephant, without saying a word, had shown us all up. With a few curious steps, he had laid our souls bare, now it was up to us to take the next step. Hopefully it would not be to run away.

Guests Say the Darnedest Things

The inevitable mixing of cultures and languages is one of the rewards of guiding at 'high-end' safari camps. 'Lost in translation' incidents can be frustrating and entertaining in roughly equal measures.

On a Namibian trip our small group joined a French couple on a game drive at a lodge near the spectacular red dunes of Sossusvlei. It was the Parisians' second night and they were thoroughly enjoying the experience. They had a great rapport with the resident guide and had seen a fair amount of desert-adapted wildlife such as springbok, gemsbok, Hartmann's Mountain Zebra, meerkats and a porcupine. We had had much the same experience that afternoon, except of course for the nocturnal porcupine, and after our sundowner stop, the guide explained the purpose and ethics of the red-filtered spotlight and suggested we might be lucky enough to see species like aardwolf, Bat-eared Fox and horny bugger. At least that is how the French lady understood the statement and proudly regaled us in her thick accent about the profligate mating habits of porcupines who, she said, needed to mate on a daily basis in order to induce ovulation in the female.

We were indeed lucky enough to see a Honey Badger on that evening drive and the sighting and the repetition of the species' name clarified the earlier conversation in all of our minds and resulted in much uproarious laughter and good-natured teasing about *amour*.

Chris Roche

Monstrous Mammals

(North of the Timbavati River, South Africa)

by DAVID HOOD

Considerable Cats

'That's the biggest lion I've ever seen! . . . He's big, isn't he?'

'Quite big,' I nod, as a young male lion, his mane mere fluff, walks down the road in our direction. He pads slowly towards our open Land Rover without looking at us or acknowledging us.

There is another vehicle behind us and there is no place on either side of the road to move to. We are stuck and I cannot move out of his way. He continues determinedly towards us. I turn my head to see how the guests are reacting to his approach.

Horst is practically sitting on Brigitt's lap on the seat behind me. The other four guests are all wide-eyed and open-mouthed. That is a normal reaction when you are in fear of your life. Opening your mouth allows you to hear slightly better – important when you are straining your senses to assess a lethal danger. I glance at my tracker, Simeon, who is sitting in the passenger seat next to me. He is flipping absentmindedly through my bird book.

I want to put the guests at their ease. I want to explain why we are not in danger. I want to tell them about how we have observed this lion since he was a tiny cub and have thus gained some knowledge of his temperament. I want to explain that lions simply do not jump into vehicles where they are not fed from them. Finally I'd like to mention that he is going somewhere else and the road just happens to be the easiest path. Even if they are not entirely convinced, perhaps it would be of some comfort.

The lion, however, is not about to wait in the road while I explain these nuances of animal behaviour to my petrified guests. Instead, I turn to them, smile and manage a reasonably confident, 'It's all right!'

I whisper this paraphrase of my good intentions in an excited tone. I am trying to convince them that this is a great experience rather than their final one. This might help on an intellectual level, but as the lion closes in their brains are receiving more powerful, conflicting signals. These signals are travelling at lightning speed along neural pathways ingrained in their genetic makeup. Subconsciously, images from a primal dream are flicking through their brains, desperately searching for a response to the approaching predator. Pure fear courses powerfully through veins driven by adrenaline-fuelled hearts.

Meanwhile, as if in slow motion, the lion is placing one relentless padded paw in front of another. His head is hanging heavily as if he is a little tired. His tail does a sharp flick as he waves off a fly. At less than a vehicle's length from us, he steps off the road. This is the first physical acknowledgement of our presence that I have noticed. He continues toward Simeon's side of the vehicle.

Horst sidles back to his side of the vehicle, followed closely by Brigitt. Behind them, the other two couples edge stiffly away from the side of the Land Rover in unison. They are no longer high-powered business-men and women. They are little antelope with dubious amounts of self-awareness, huddled together, watching the big cat with a clarity of vision they will lose as soon as full conscious thought returns.

Simeon looks up between the cuckoos and coucals as the lion draws level with the bull bars. The robust carnivore is moving past us, giving us a berth of no more than a metre. His shoulder blades are undulating beneath a coat of rough, tawny hair. Brigitt registers the sound of dry grass crumpling beneath tough pads. She will remember neither that sound nor the scar under the big cat's left eye, which she saw clearly.

He still has not deigned to look up at us and continues, without breaking stride, to similarly terrorise the guests in the vehicle behind us. They, at least, have the comfort of seeing us survive the ordeal. And

then he is gone. He leaves no sign of his passing save the raucous staccato alarm call of a Swainson's Spurfowl that he surprises.

Simeon closes the book at the Pipits.

Once he has started to breathe again, Horst comments: 'Zat vos vewy close vosn't it?'

'It was close,' I agree, and Brigitt consents silently with furious nods.

Zack, a Texan, continues his earlier train of thought from the second row back, 'That was without a doubt the biggest male lion that I have ever laid eyes upon!' He pauses. 'Have you ever seen a lion that big, Anne-Marie?' He looks hard at his wife.

'It sure was big!' she replies.

'Grande!' confirms Donna, from the back.

I try to put his size in perspective. 'They are big animals,' I say, 'he's still a young lion though, about two years old, did you see how his mane was just starting to grow?' I pause and there are a few nods. I continue, 'He'll get quite a bit bigger, lions usually reach a maximum weight at about seven years. Soon after that their condition gradually deteriorates. His mane will keep growing though, and its condition can give a rough indication of his history. If he stays healthy and well fed he'll have a bigger, better looking mane than if he struggles to find food.'

But Zack is not to be deterred. 'If he's gonna get bigger, he's gonna be one mean old lion! I don't believe those lions we saw in Kenya were anywhere near as big as this fellow.' He looks again at Anne-Marie.

'They sure weren't, and those lions we saw in Botswana were scrawny by comparison!' Anne-Marie recounts.

'Oh, they were *scrawny* lions!' Zack agrees.

I smile secretly, knowing that the next time Zack goes on safari, he will quite likely see even *bigger* lions. The young male that had walked past us was somewhere between two thirds and three quarters the weight he would eventually reach and he was by no means exceptional.

Zack's response was normal. I understood it. Lions affected people that way. At countless sightings I have marvelled at the same response.

A viewer unaccustomed to seeing lions at close range can always be forgiven for having unrealistic expectations of their size. The shattering of these expectations when one of these mighty beasts rises to their feet after a doze can by no means be considered unusual.

But that's not it. A simple lack of familiarity cannot explain it away. I have frequently been startled by similar responses from seasoned safari-goers and other rangers. Comments such as: 'These are seriously big lions!', or 'I reckon these lions are a lot bigger than the ones in Zimbabwe!'

What's going on, I think to myself, exasperated. *Is it just me?* And if I reply, sarcastically, 'I've never heard anyone look at a lion and say, "That's quite a small lion!" or, "This lion is rather average."' I am invariably answered with suspicious stares.

Yet, there is something about them that is larger than life. Perhaps our exaggerated impressions of size are a reaction to a quality of presence we are unable to fully comprehend. There is much about lions that is incompatible with honourable western ideals. We find the brutal ferocity that resides behind their eyes and in their movement inexplicably attractive, but mostly we have forgotten what it is to be a killer. Few people are able to reconcile the cute cubs tackling one another on the soft riverbed sand with the hungry killers ripping into the warm flesh of a zebra's haunch. We smile when the lazy lioness rolls onto her back, letting her floppy paws hang. Yet when that same female pulls her bloody head from the abdominal cavity of a freshly killed wildebeest, we cringe. We feel the bile rising in our throats when we see she is holding a fully formed foetus between her teeth. The carnal nature of a lion is savage. They are purists. Pure killers. Purely selfish. The blood of innocents is their life.

There comes a point where we choose no longer to understand. Sometimes the disillusionment of our own nurtured principles would be too harsh if we went any further.

And so we leave the lion, lying in the tall grass. We turn our backs and walk away in search of solace. We will find it in the sunset, but first there is another animal we cannot simply walk past.

Modern-day Mammoths

The elephant shares with the lion the ability to confuse the senses. No matter how we interpret their size, elephants are big!

As a young boy, I was promised a trip to the Addo Elephant National Park. Here I was to see the first of these pachyderms I would be able to remember. The trip was delayed due to the weather and the elephants grew ever taller in my imagination. On pillar-like legs they towered above the trees, holding my destiny in the soles of their feet. From the windows of our tiny car I could see only the tree trunks of their legs. I held my breath as I waited upon their verdict.

Since then elephants have become a lot smaller for me, but one dark night in the lowveld I was reminded, once again, that elephants *are* big.

I was taking two guests on a game drive that evening – two adventurous ladies who were taking some time out together. It had not been dark long and we were on our way to find a place to stop for a drink, before heading back to the lodge. At night, it is preferable to stop in an open area if you are going to get out of the vehicle. With that in mind, I was headed for a clearing I knew of, when we came upon an elephant. He was walking along the road ahead of us.

Earlier that day we had seen an elephant not too far from there. The animal ahead of us turned out to be the same one. We knew from watching him earlier that he was an older bull, heavily in musth.* Because he was in this condition, we kept a safe distance and observed him for a while. He was trudging steadily along the road without stopping to feed as he had been doing earlier.

A bull in musth does that, he walks for extended periods, calling and listening. He is hoping to hear from a female in a herd, particularly a female in oestrus. Such a female probably has a distinct infrasonic call. As the bull walks, he dribbles copious amounts of urine. His urine at this time has a powerful smell. A herd of females coming across this scent may actually follow the trail in search of him.

---

*   A periodical condition, particularly in older bulls, during which testosterone levels are highly elevated. Musth is indicated by a secretion from the temporal gland, situated behind the animal's eye, and a particularly pungent odour. Musth bulls can be more aggressive and less predictable than normal.

This elephant was definitely hogging the road. I knew that less than a kilometre ahead there was a four-way junction. We could have turned around at this point and gone around another way, but waiting until the elephant got to the junction would be just as quick. We followed him at a distance varying between about seventy and a hundred metres. He took no notice of us, so we trundled along behind him as he plodded, neither determinedly nor wistfully.

The road descended towards a small dry riverbed and we lost sight of him as the track angled downward and curved slightly. I slowed down a little, unable to see the elephant and unwilling to get too close. As the dip came into view, there was the elephant. He was already on the other side of the riverbed and continuing his unhurried march along the road. We crossed the soft sand of the riverbed and followed him at our earlier respectful distance. At least, I believed it to be respectful . . .

He plodded. We trundled. He still had not turned to look at us. We had been following him for at least five minutes now. In another minute or two we would be at the junction.

We were enjoying this. The elephant's steady, wrinkle-bottomed walk became almost comical if you watched it for long enough. The track was ascending slowly and to prevent erosion on slopes such as this, humps had been made. The humps were angled slightly to direct rainwater off the road. The elephant went up a hump and down the other side. Moments later, we followed, up and over.

A short furrow had been graded next to each hump to direct the water a little further away from the road. Where it had been graded, a small clearing had been created by the bulldozer. Other than these gaps, visibility through the dense bush was extremely low. A few small, wiry mopane trees formed a clump next to the long bow-shaped branches of White Raisins. These trees have no trunk and all the branches originate in a tight cluster on the ground before curving upwards a little higher than a Land Rover. Bushwillows too, reflected the spotlight with green and gold leaves while small spiky *Acacia*s filled the gaps. Above this mosaic of small trees, the rough branches of larger Knob Thorns and patchwork boughs of marulas rose into the night. Every one of these provided food for elephant, but he was not interested. He kept plodding and listening. We kept trundling and watching.

The elephant must have been just less than a hundred metres from us when he turned. He turned quickly, and silently he charged.

Many visitors to game reserves tell tales of terrifying elephant charges. I believe that in nearly all of these cases, had they just waited, the elephant would have stopped a good distance from them, perhaps shaken its head with ears spread, and backed off. With limited experience of elephant behaviour, and even with considerable experience, it is always wise to be the first to back off. In fact, you often find yourself doing so before you have had a chance to properly contemplate the options. However, when you do start moving away, the elephant, often a young bull, triumphantly presses his advantage by following the vehicle. Elephants do exactly the same to other animals.

This was different.

As the elephant charged, I watched, and time slowed down. Adrenaline kicked in – certainly the elephant had surprised me but I was not terrified. I recognised something different in his behaviour and I was fascinated.

Meanwhile, my tracker, who was perched on the seat at the front of the vehicle, was signalling frantically with the spotlight for me to move the now stationary vehicle. A man of few words, he simply told me to go. 'Famba,' he said, and then louder, 'Famba!'

This broke my reverie and options flashed through my mind. The elephant had halved the distance and turning around or reversing would not be fast enough. Nor am I certain that any amount of shouting and clapping would have stopped him. We were in trouble.

My tracker was waving the spotlight towards one of the small clearings where a furrow had been bulldozed.

The elephant was massive. He was coming down the slope and he was in full charge. He was not waiting to see what we would do. I put my foot down hard on the pedal and we accelerated towards the elephant.

And turned into the furrow-clearing.

And into a White Raisin tree.

The spindly branches buckled and snapped as the Land Rover forced its way into them. On my right, a raging elephant bull cut the corner towards us. I looked up at him. He was now less than twenty metres away. My tracker was still bravely waving the spotlight in the direction he thought I should go. He tried to move his legs to the side but there was no escaping the tough branches that whipped at his legs and body. I have no idea what the guests were doing.

I could not see more than a couple of metres beyond the front of the vehicle but my foot was down flat and my prayer was that there were no big Knob Thorns lurking ahead. With the visibility I had, I would not have had time to avoid them. It was a risk I had to take.

We smashed over a bushwillow and through a small opening into another White Raisin. Snapped branchlets and dislodged leaves showered the vehicle. We crashed on through the foliage, guessing, hoping. My tracker held on with one hand as the vehicle bounced over unseen ruts and holes in the ground. His other hand held the spotlight, which flickered across the darkness illuminating more obstacles as he continued to direct me.

Then the bush began to open up. Sensing that the elephant was no longer there, I slowed down. My tracker, scratched and scraped as he had been, appeared to be in one piece. I was thankful for that. I turned to see how the two ladies were. 'He's gone!' they confirmed from the back seat. I could not see their expressions in the dark. It dawned on me then that they would have been able to see the elephant a whole lot closer from up there than I had.

I asked how they were. They said they were all right, but I think they were being brave. Nevertheless, I decided that rather than heading straight back to the lodge, we should stop for a drink. This would give us a chance to discuss the elephant charge and try to understand it. I did not want my guests to develop an unnecessary dread of elephants.

'Would you like a drink?' I asked.

'Definitely!'

We stopped in a clearing and set up our table with a spread of drinks and snacks in the Land Rover's headlights.

'Rebecca, what will you have to drink?' I asked.

'Whisky please.'

'Double or single?'

'Double!' she stated emphatically and we all laughed, releasing some of the tension.

'Tina?'

'Double whisky will be just fine!'

With drinks in our hands and the stars above our heads we all agreed that it had been a really big elephant.

Although a little shaken, I was surprised at how well they had handled the incident. They explained to me how the elephant had come to just a few metres behind the vehicle. It was pretty scary, but apart from watching the elephant, they had been watching me. Of course they had! They thought I looked calm enough, so they assumed it was all under control.

In many ways I had surprised myself in that respect, I had been completely calm, but my lack of fear frightened me. That sort of fear keeps us safe. I must never lose it. At the same time I realised that no matter what sort of empathy I thought I had with elephants, I had hardly begun to understand them.

To this day, that remains the case. Every time I misjudge the size of an elephant, I wonder if it is not their bulk, but something deeper that is confusing me.

Later that evening we arrived back at the lodge. Rebecca and Tina went to their rooms to freshen up before dinner. I took my rifle and book bag and thanked my tracker for his invaluable help. I realise now that if he had not hurried me on, things may have turned out differently and I am indebted.

I was about to say goodnight when he stopped me.

'Mfo,' he said, 'do you mind if I take one vodka from the box?'

I thought for a moment, 'Go ahead, mfo.'

He had never made such a request before and never did again. I smiled as I walked away, but deep down I was frightened, once again, by my own lack of fear. I wanted it back, but really, I knew where it had gone.

That's Another Story.

Lend Me Your Ears

One of the things that is particularly striking about the Greater Kudu is the size and prominent position of its ears. They are enormous. When some physical feature is so apparent, it is in our nature to want an explanation. The most common – and most obvious – explanation is that it improves the animal's hearing. It is said that because kudu spend a lot of time in thicker bush, they need to be able to hear danger where they may not be able to see it. Of course they do – but why then are the little duikers not adorned with such enormous appendages, or the kudu's close relative, the bushbuck – they too prefer a habitat of thick bush.

Another antelope that is known for its large ears is the little steenbok, but the steenbok avoids woodland and forest, spending most of its time in very open terrain, which, through an extension of this logic, would surely mean that it would not need such good hearing.

A careful look at a kudu's ears backlit in the evening light reveals a very pink colour on their inner surface. Just like a hare's ears, a network of fine blood vessels close to the surface gives this colour. Interestingly, both the kudu and the steenbok can survive without water, and both species have a wide distribution range extending into some of the hotter, more arid areas of the continent. In these environments, temperature control becomes a real issue.

The most effective way for any animal to avoid heat stress is to take advantage of the cooling effect of evaporation. Usually this means losing water by panting or through the nasal passages. For animals like kudu and steenbok, living in dry areas where water conservation is paramount, an alternative means of cooling such as convection across a large surface area (such as its ears) may be a crucial adaptation to avoid dehydration while keeping body temperature down.

Being able to function in this manner allows an animal more freedom of habitat choice. Another of the kudu's cousins, the nyala, may have other constraints on the habitat types it is able to exploit, but it too has big ears and it too can survive without water where none is available. Consequently it is able to utilize food sources far from water that other animals cannot reach. Like the kudu, it prefers a more densely vegetated habitat, particularly riverine bush.

So too, the Cape Hare, with its enormous ears, has been shown to be able to survive without water for extended periods. By contrast, the Sitatunga, another relative of the kudu, is highly adapted to wetlands and swampy reedbeds, never venturing far from water and it has much smaller ears.

Lastly the elephant deserves a mention. Being so big it has a problem with overheating as the heat it generates metabolically has so much further to go to escape its body. It does need to drink – a lot – but in addition it uses its ears as an effective cooling device. This device has been studied in the giant pachyderm and some astounding figures have been recorded.

The surface area of an elephant's ears makes up an amazing twenty per cent of its total body surface area. Six litres of blood can be pumped through each ear every minute and by doing this and flapping its ears to get airflow over the massive veins on their hind surfaces, an elephant can lose nearly two thirds of its body heat through its ears alone.

If that is what the elephant can do with its ears then perhaps it is not unreasonable to imagine that the big ears of the kudu and the steenbok have developed to give those animals an edge that is not just about hearing things that sneak around in the dark.

David Hood

The Rules

by DAVID HOOD

There are many rules that go along with guiding. Some of these rules are not negotiable. For instance, if you were to accidentally fire a shot after loading your rifle, that would not be OK. Other rules are open to interpretation and the source of much heated debate between rangers. High on this list would be the topic of driving off-road. Rules describing a lodge's policy on such a topic might read something like: *Off-road driving should be done in a sensitive manner. Off-road driving should not be done on areas susceptible to erosion. There will be no off-road driving after heavy rain and until the designated head ranger declares the ground dry enough to resume this practice.*

The sliding scale of sensitivity can be and often is squeezed to its limits. It is easy to do when your six sullen German guests have stopped talking to you much and fail entirely to respond to your enthusiastic monologues on medicinal trees. At this point the only communication you are getting from their side is: 'Ve vant to see da lee-o-pard!' You know there is one down in the riverbed because you've heard it called in on the radio. Problem is: You won't have time to drive around to the river crossing and up the sandy riverbed because your guests have a flight to Hamburg awaiting them. However if you just drive down the steep, erosion-sensitive riverbank you can fit in a lee-o-pard before rushing back to the lodge for a quick coffee before the trip to the airport. You will have a far more pleasant drive home and possibly even some tips. After all, the guests are paying lots of money to *see* animals, aren't they?

In hindsight, you should never have driven down that bank, but at the time it seemed like the best option and perhaps that section of the bank was not all that 'erosion sensitive'. Perhaps it was.

Those rules can all be found on paper. It's the other rules that I am going to tell you about now: the unwritten rules, the ranger's secret, personal codes. These are the rules that must *never* be broken. A ranger's dignity is at stake here, the essence of his being would be shaken should these vows be compromised.

Rule One: Never Swear Loudly on a Game Drive
(The Okavango, Northern Botswana)

In Botswana you are not necessarily trained or taught anything. You simply do it. So it was with my guiding career there. I was simply asked: 'Can you do a game drive this afternoon?' And I simply answered: 'No problem.'

Immediately I cursed my own stupidity. Did I not realise that three hours of driving around seven thousand hectares is not enough to get to know it really well? Was I not conscious of the fact that as I had only been there three days and was not employed as a guide, I was entitled to decline?

In Botswana I had became a sun worshipper, always staring up at its incandescence, marvelling at its ability to guide me home. The endless wild places of the Okavango Delta are flat. There is not a single hill, ridge or rise in its expanse to act as a landmark. The whole area was once an enormous inland sea. Today you will not find a single rock jutting up from beneath the sandy soils of the Delta's spread. The only rocks lie hundreds of metres below the surface, covered in millennia of sandy deposits. Consequently, in the absence of any landmarks, I would head out from the lodge in one direction, keeping in as straight a line as I could and return in exactly the opposite direction.

After a few days, my initial north-south game drives began to take on a bit more variety and I soon began to enjoy myself, confident that I had a good chance of finding the lodge again. I was fortunate to be able to share with my guests that wonderful experience of driving through entirely new and unfamiliar terrain.

A few weeks later, Greg and Lindsay arrived at our little camp. They were a lovely South African couple, young, not married long and pleasantly easy-going. I was called upon from the midst of servicing Land-cruisers, fixing pumps and painting things to be their guide. 'No problem,' I said.

Greg and Lindsay loved the bush; they had been to reserves in South Africa before and were excited to see whatever treasures our concession held in store for them. We set off on a game drive, admiring the beautiful scenery and enjoying the prospect of exciting adventures to come. I stopped to show them the Wild Sage plant so abundant in our area and explained how it could be used as an effective insect repellent. Afterwards I threw a couple of branches at my feet. This was to prevent the tsetse flies from biting me and making it seem as though I couldn't drive very well. We looked at a few birds and wondered at the hamer-kop's extravagant nest. We watched tsessebe making their way across a dry floodplain and closer to the water studied Red Lechwe as they grazed and then ran with heads lowered. In the distance giraffe ambled across the plains in slow motion. It was a pleasant afternoon and we enjoyed the sunset over a cold drink, before climbing back into the Landcruiser for the night drive and the journey back.

It was after dark when I found myself, as I often did in those days, on a road I had not intended to be on. This road would lead me to some far-flung corner of the concession if I stayed on it. Turning around, although sensible, never seemed like the best course, particularly as I had apparently managed to convince Greg and Lindsay that I knew this vast wilderness like the back of my hand. There were two other choices. I could take another road further along and simply loop back the way I had come. I considered this option whilst still heading steadily north. As I was already out later than normal, this would mean getting back to the lodge very late, so I decided on the second option.

The second option involved a short cut. The short cut was a perfectly good road through a lot of mopane that had simply not been used for some time due to a deep, and therefore treacherous, water crossing at its beginning. The water level had been subsiding but there was still a considerable danger that elephants had pushed over trees in the mopane forest, as they often did, blocking the road in the process. I decided to risk it.

We were not far from the crossing now, so I took the turn that led there and in no time at all we were faced with a dark expanse of sluggishly flowing water. The Landcruiser's lights bounced off its glossy surface reflecting patterns into the mopane trees on the other side. I judged by the width of the water that it would be a bit deeper than the top of the wheels. If I kept going through it at a steady speed, it should be fine. Water would splash over the bonnet but the momentum of the vehicle would ensure a temporary air pocket around the engine, keeping the vital electrics dry. The danger was that water would get into the connections between the distributor and the leads that conduct electricity to the spark plugs, disrupting the flow of current and causing the engine to misfire.

I looked at my watch. Eight o'clock exactly. The other guests would be safely back at the lodge by now, probably waiting for us to get back before they took their seats for the first course. I engaged low range second gear, smiled reassuringly at Greg and Lindsay and edged forward towards the water. Although my heart was beating heavily in my chest, the familiar sound of water sloshing around the wheels was somehow comforting. I had done this many times before, I reminded myself. The pitch of the sloshing changed as the bodywork dipped into the water.

A bow wave began to form around the front part of the vehicle. As the water deepened, the lights that had been reflecting ripples onto the grassy slopes and reedbeds of the opposite bank disappeared beneath the bow wave, creating an eerie underwater glow. Greg and Lindsay, holding on tight, were enjoying the ride.

Beneath the bonnet the cooling fan, designed to keep air moving over the hot engine block, was spinning in accordance with the high revs I was making the engine do. As the water deepened, the bottom of the fan was plunged into the cool liquid. Pure Okavango water began to spray backwards over hot metal.

Clutching the steering wheel tightly, I was doing my best to estimate where the underwater road should be. My heart sank when I felt the first stutter of the engine. I kept going though, trying to maintain a steady pace. The Landcruiser had six cylinders and even if water splashed onto one of the connections, short-circuiting current to one cylinder, I could keep going on the other five.

The final stutter happened somewhere near the middle of the crossing. My legs began to get wet as water rushed into the footwell. A number of points registered at once in my mind:

1) We were stuck in a river.
2) We were far from the lodge, or any human habitation for that matter.
3) The radio probably didn't work this far from the lodge in a dip such as the one we were in.
4) If by some miracle the radio did work, no-one would be in the office at this time to hear it.
5) My veldskoens were wet.
6) Anyone who came searching for us would not suspect we were here.
7) It would be a long walk – in wet veldskoens.

All of this I could sum up in one four-letter word, shouted to the wilderness. As the echoes of my cry died down, I remembered Greg and Lindsay . . .

This story does have a happy ending however. After feeling extremely ashamed of myself and apologising for my unruly language, I got to work. Greg and Lindsay meanwhile appeared unaware that I had broken any rules and were relatively unperturbed by the gently flowing, crocodile-inhabited water around them. After opening the bonnet and confirming that the distributor was underwater and failing to get any response on the radio, I paused to consider the situation more carefully. That was when a revelation came to me.

I had often started vehicles in gear – unintentionally of course – and knew what happened when you did so. I had heard of the power of the starter motor spoken about amongst wannabe mechanics. Why not give it a try, I thought? 'Hold on,' I cried, engaged reverse, turned and held the key. The vehicle jerked backwards and kept jerking backwards. I held the key just long enough to get us onto slightly higher ground. I could then dry out the electrical parts and spray oil onto the connections before reversing the rest of the way out and onto dry land.

I seemed to have redeemed myself in Greg and Lindsay's eyes. In fact, they seemed to take it all in their stride as one big adventure. We were all happy to go back the way we'd come but my relief was mixed with disappointment. I had broken rule number one.

Rule Two: Never Laugh at a Guest
(The Lowveld, South Africa)

> The perception of a leopard is always incomplete. It moves through the shadows of our imagination, never wholly visible. Its shape is obscured by the swathes of brown grass or the branches of the Jackal-berry tree. When it walks across a clearing it is careful not to linger long enough to let our eyes grasp the complexity of its spots. Like a true cat, it owns those who find it rather than the other way around. It has claimed many who have seen it. Even those who have been fortunate enough to spend time with it will always remain hungry for more of its mysteries.

If a ranger has a favourite animal, it is usually the leopard. I refuse, for now, to be part of the mass, but secretly, on some level, I agree.

On a safari, the leopard is often the most difficult of the big game to find and the unticked number five of many an intrepid safari-goer's list. And so it was that after conversing with my newly arrived guests, I found that the leopard was one of the animals they hoped to see.

They had come at a good time because that morning the trackers had found a female leopard. She had been feeding on an impala kill, which she had hoisted into a large marula tree. As there was still plenty of meat left on the impala, there was a good chance that she would remain in the area.

She did and not two hours into our game drive we were parked amongst the soft leaves of a bushwillow studying the leopard in the marula tree. It was a warm, peaceful afternoon. Chinspot Batises and hornbills provided pleasant background sounds while the faint buzzing of flies could be heard around the carcass. A faint breeze cooled us from time to time as it rustled through the leaves around us and caused the dry grass to wave its fingers at the blue sky overhead. We had stopped about ten metres from the shadow of the marula tree and had a good view up into its solid boughs. The leopard lay panting on one of these branches alternating its piercing gaze between us, the impala on a near-by branch and the far-off distance.

I had just begun to touch on a few points of leopard behaviour in between enjoying the beautiful sight when the South African guest behind me attracted my attention. Looking up at the bloody remains of the cat's prey, she made a most astounding observation . . .

'Look David,' she whispered, 'there's an impala up there too. I never knew impala could climb trees!'

There was a long moment of silence. And then a raucous laugh burst from my lips.

She turned a little pink but this time I did not apologise.

Rule Three: Never Hoot on Game Drive
(Somewhere South of the Hoanib Riverbed, Damaraland)

Hooting is barbaric. The only times when hooting could possibly be condoned in everyday life are to warn someone about to drive into you, or to bid farewell when driving away from the house of long-lost friends.

In the bush it is taboo. In most reserves the hooters are actually disconnected so that even if you desperately need to hoot, you can't.

Being in a wilderness area is in many ways a spiritual experience. Spending time with wild animals can reawaken our tired souls. That is why loud noises such as hooters and ringing cell phones are sacrilegious.

I had been asked to help guide a trip in Damaraland, northwest Namibia. The main focus of this safari was to track and view a Desert Black Rhinoceros . . . on foot. Here, extra water, a GPS and good boots ranked among the most important items of equipment. After driving for most of the day, we arrived at the first camp after sunset. The camp included a few rudimentary shelters and some levelled pieces of ground for pitching tents. It was dwarfed by a massive shelf of rock that stretched up into space just behind the beautifully named Elephant Song camp. Tents were hurriedly pitched in the disappearing twilight and dinner was prepared.

Now that the day was coming to a close, I had a few moments to think while I hungrily wolfed down dinner. I realised something I had been denying up till then. This was going to be a *long* safari. Our guests were going to make it that way. Don, a tall, lanky man from the United States, was particular. The desert is no place to be particular, but Don *was* particular and he had a particular skin problem for which he needed extra water for washing. Water was one thing we did *not* have extra of. We had to carry most of the water we would use in with us, squeezed between tents, cooking equipment, cool boxes, and Don's little Asian wife Phong's luggage.

The other two guests were both British. They were on honeymoon after a second marriage. Unfortunately Sasha got carsick. As the fact that much of our waking time on this safari was to be spent in vehicles, travelling the vast distances, dawned on her new husband, he began to find other things to complain about.

To complete this picture, the previous two days' experiences need to be mentioned: After travelling non-stop across the Kalahari, driving day and night, we arrived at the backpackers where we intended to stay. It was well after dark and we were weary and hungry. I decided to have a shower before dinner. On my return to the dormitory, I was asked to wait outside for a little bit because someone on the other side of the door had cut his throat! It was a failed attempt, but the poor girl who was hostess and co-organiser on our trip had witnessed more than me and did not sleep easily for the next few nights. The next day we discovered that the company we had planned to hire a lot of our equipment from had fallen short on their promises, failing to produce such essential items as tents. Later that day, one of the vehicles we had hired was broken into. There were a string of delays involving the replacement vehicle, which culminated in our late start.

At Elephant Song, the expedition leader explained the plans for the next few days to the guests and they trundled off to beds full of desert apprehensions. We, together with our newly acquired tracker for the trip, washed up and looked for places to put our sleeping mats. After checking for scorpions, mats were unrolled and a long day had officially ended. The call of a Spotted Eagle Owl and the splendour of the stars above overwhelmed me. The hectic preparations and unexpected events of the previous days slipped into insignificance as the desert night took over. My only concern was the fact that I could actually smell myself. Yes, there was no denying it. I vowed to find enough water to wash the next morning and closed my eyes.

The next day started off cheerfully enough, or was that just my anticipation of the strange wonders to come? Certainly the guests seemed more wary than they had been in their guesthouse the previous night.

We packed up and with Sasha and her husband, Gerald, in my charge, set off into some of the most barren landscape imaginable. The harshness of rocks was broken only by the sinuous thread of a dry riverbed. We joined up with this and began to follow the course of its flat, sandy bottom west towards the land of endless red rocks. Small trees and thick-leaved bushes made the banks of the riverbed their unlikely home. Beyond them the angular hills were bare except for clumps of dry grass and succulent plants. We began to see the fleshy *Euphorbia damarensis* favoured by our elusive quarry, the Black Rhino. Further down the riverbed the vegetation began to change subtly and soon we were rewarded with the sight of enormous ana trees. These are closely related to *Acacia* trees and their solid trunks and rounded crowns dwarfed our white Nissan four-by-fours, a handful of which could have easily parked in their dappled shade.

Still transfixed by the scenery, I came around a corner to see the other vehicle stopped in the riverbed ahead . . . and elephants! We were hoping to see them, but in the vastness of Damaraland, I had little faith that we really would. Yet there they were, real Desert Elephants.

These fascinating creatures, I explained to Gerald and Sasha in a low voice, were very different from their savannah-dwelling relatives. They were a little smaller and generally had straighter tusks. They spent much of their time close to these riverbeds during the dry winter, moving further afield in the warmer months when rain caused hardy grasses to sprout fresh growth.

The elephants were watching us. A small group of females with young of various sizes moved onto the glaring riverbed ahead of us. Flapping their ears heavily, they looked across the white sand at our vehicles. Closer to hand, a young bull looked down on us from the raised riverbank. For minutes, all eight in our party were captivated by these desert giants. The air was still and starting to heat up. Massive ana trees framed the distant elephant and rocky slopes dwarfed even the trees.

I explained to our guests how the behaviour of these elephants differed remarkably from their counterparts in better-vegetated areas. Unlike other elephants, known for their wasteful eating habits, these animals seemed to know that food was limited and seldom pushed over trees or broke off big branches.

We watched the young bull up on the bank as he moved towards us. His bulk disappeared behind a small thicket. We waited. The group in the riverbed had crossed onto the opposite bank and a little one ran to catch up as its mother vanished behind a bush. The bull moved forward enough for us to see his head. He waited there for some time, watching us with an unfathomable eye. After a little while, he came down into the riverbed, right in front of us, and stopped again. We were all breathless.

After we had enjoyed this sight for some time, I turned to whisper some juicy information about elephant morphology to Gerald and Sasha. I turned in my seat so that I could see them, at the same time placing a significant portion of my body weight against the middle of the steering wheel. Right where the hooter was! In many ways, I have to say, it was a 'safari from hell'.

Seventeen Years in Brothels

Standing in the cool under the reception's thatch, waiting for an airport transport to arrive mid-morning is as much a part of ranger life as guiding safaris. So too is making final, casual chitchat with the waiting guests before they depart.

An Englishman beside me, overhearing a French couple nearby, turns to them and engages in brief pleasantries. Turning back to me, he asks privately, 'I suppose you're wondering why I can speak French?' and without waiting for a reply continues, 'I lived in brothels for seventeen years'.

Just a little startled by this blatant declaration, I nod my head in the appropriate diplomatic manner, backing my confused and somewhat embarrassed disposition up with a quiet, 'Oh, I see,' as if everything was quite normal.

A little later, the very proper English gentleman again turns to me and says, 'Do you want to know why I needed to learn French?' To which I reply, 'No, I'm rather more curious as to why you lived in brothels for seventeen years.'

An outburst of hysterical laughter leaves me feeling even more sheepish. 'No, no, I said I lived in Brussels for seventeen years!'

Megan Emmett

Snake Stories: Silly, Serious and Sublime

by CHRIS ROCHE

S nakes are an intrinsic part of the bush and, by extension, every guide's life. Everyone has a story of the most venomous snake they have had to remove from a guest's room, the kitchen fridge, or other favourite reptilian retreats. We have all also missed standing on Puff Adders by mere inches and been reared at by the biggest Black Mamba, which lay stretched right across the road and then some. Some of us have even been bitten and evacuated to hospital. In amongst all this lot though, there are some genuinely funny snake encounters.

Imitation is the Sincerest Form of Flattery
(Sabi Sand Game Reserve, South Africa)

A perennial entertainment, for big groups of conference or incentive guests using lodges in the South African lowveld, is to bring a snake handler and snakes in from outside the reserve as a kind of educational thrill for guests and staff alike. It's here that guides often learn the rudiments of snake handling, the more adventurous among them soon putting this into practice on game drives. So it was that one Clint Steyn*, a guide of some experience at a well known lodge in the Sabi Sand Wildtuin, decided to experiment with his newly acquired skills one afternoon.

Clint and his tracker, Petrus Sithole, were well known in the area for being able to locate lion and leopard when others could not. They

---

* All names have been changed to prevent embarrassment!

had a great friendship and working relationship and always kept guests entertained and informed with their blend of experience, wit and repartee. This afternoon they were not looking for anything in particular but just a kilometre from camp happened across a Puff Adder crossing the road. Petrus and Clint quickly jumped out of the vehicle and approached the slowly moving snake. It halted its rectilinear movement across the vehicle track and contemplated its adversary. Clint and Petrus in turn contemplated each other and instantly began some good-natured banter about who should pick it up and so demonstrate that he had graduated from non-venomous species. Clint lost the coin flip.

With a stick he managed to hold down the snake and nervously used his thumb and forefinger to pick it up behind the head. Holding it up for the impressed guests to see, Clint warmed to the occasion and talked the guests through the erectile fangs and cytotoxic venom peculiar to the Viperinae. All was going well and he relaxed as he placed the snake back down on the edge of the road. As he did so the adder wriggled and bit him on the index finger.

His back was turned to the guests and Clint, despite the instant and intense pain, pretended that nothing was amiss. Not even Petrus had noticed the bite and the party moved on to watch a female leopard on the opposite side of the concession to the lodge. During this time Clint's whole hand and then his entire forearm swelled enormously, forcing him to drive and change gear with his left hand – something that the guests couldn't help but notice. The incident now out in the open, Clint soldiered on, too stubborn to cut the drive short. As soon as they got back to the lodge though he headed off to the nearest city – three hours' drive away – where he spent the next ten days in hospital . . .

'No, really, I'm fine. Do you think you could reach the radio mic?'
(Maputaland, South Africa)

In much the same circumstances, another young guide at a reserve in northern KwaZulu-Natal was driving through a patch of spectacular

Sand Forest when his tracker pointed out a small Southern African Python lying still in the middle of the road. Pythons are spectacularly beautiful snakes and the guide, Paul, took the opportunity to get off the vehicle and catch the metre and a half long reptile.

No sooner had he caught it behind the head than the python began to coil itself around his right arm. Not unduly worried, he reached down with his left hand to begin unwinding the snake. The python suddenly struck at his left hand, managing to engulf it in its mouth. This was a little sore, the python's curved teeth digging deeply into the flesh of Paul's hand. Every attempt to pull against the curve of the teeth resulted in more pain, but any let up of pressure allowed the snake to further consolidate its grip and continue to swallow Paul's hand.

Rather than calm, professional and unflappable, the guide was now visibly concerned. He contemplated asking his guests, who were looking on with a mixture of bemusement and horror, to radio for help. No less concerned was the tracker, but he quickly overcame his distrust of snakes and managed to uncoil the snake and free Paul's right arm, the hand of which was now used to try and prise the python's jaws loose from their grip. Slowly but surely the python was inched backwards down Paul's left arm until a final wrench freed him and the snake.

The python was gratefully released into the undergrowth on the side of the road, presumably with some sense of moral victory, while Paul climbed back into the Land Rover, his arm lacerated and still containing the tips of some of the python's teeth. Needless to say Paul came away from the experience slightly wiser . . . and with a serious infection in his forearm.

'But I was holding it behind the head!'
(The Bushveld, Bela Bela, South Africa)

Most snakes can safely be caught and held behind the head. As long as your grip is firm the snake is unable to twist its head and bring its fangs into play. There are species, however, which can bite you without needing to wriggle free. One of these is Bibron's Burrowing Asp, otherwise known as Bibron's Stiletto, legendary as a rite of passage for learner guides.

An unobtrusive, small black snake, Bibron's Stiletto spends much of its time underground in search of burrowing mammalian and reptilian prey. It is a rarely encountered species, only found above ground at night and after rain, and for this reason, and its nondescript appearance, is not well known or easy to recognise. Some guides lucky enough to encounter the species early on in their careers, were unlucky enough not to have identified it before picking it up. One of these, Bruce Marais, was just a year into his chosen career of guiding when, en route to the town of Bela Bela (then Warmbaths) for a night off, he spotted a small dark snake in the headlights of his vehicle.

Eager to impress his female companion and curious as to the snake's identity, Bruce climbed out of the vehicle and carefully picked the snake up behind the head as he had been trained to do. He dropped it as quickly as he had caught it – a searing pain quickly spreading from his thumb into his hand.

A quick change of drivers, a short trip to the local hospital (where an attempted shot of anti-venom was sensibly resisted by our hero as this has no effect on bites of this species and can in fact be harmful to the patient) and an important lesson learned! As well as familiarising himself with Bibron's Stiletto, Bruce discovered that sympathy can be as effective an aphrodisiac as anything else.

Doppelganger Gerrhosaur
(Kruger National Park, Private Concession)

I wasn't as adventurous as the guides involved in the previous stories, but having been around 'pet' snakes from an early age, was comfortable picking them up. Small nonvenomous snakes mind you! Red-lipped, Southern Brown House and Spotted Bush Snakes are one thing, but Puff Adders, boomslangs, Mozambique Spitting Cobras and the like are another story altogether, and the only way I was picking up any of these was with a snake catcher – a long-handled contraption also referred to as a grab stick. Despite my enjoyment of handling snakes like the Red-lipped and other reptiles like Flap-necked Chameleons I soon found it incompatible with my ethics, much like the handling of nightjars blinded with spotlights and the calling up of territorial birds with a tape recording. As a consequence I stopped displaying snakes to guests and merely pointed them out from the Land Rover after my tracker and I had happened upon them or found them at night with the spotlight.

Still, I was always excited to find a dead specimen of any kind of reptile and after using it as a prop for guests, usually took it back to the lodge to be dissected. One afternoon, during a quiet period at the lodge, I was out monitoring White Rhino when I was lucky enough to come across a plated lizard that had, unfortunately, been killed by another vehicle. These large lizards are a pretty uncommon sight in the South African lowveld – one species confining itself primarily to rocky habitat, and others seeking refuge in termite mounds and other burrows – and I was grateful for the opportunity to have a closer look. The fifty centimetre long reptile was in fact a Giant Plated Lizard, a charismatic creature whose generic name, *Gerrhosaurus*, gives some inkling as to its prehistoric appearance. Its solid, weighty body and well-formed scales gave it a satisfyingly tangible feel and having satiated my initial curiosity I left the dead animal in the footwell next to me and continued with the original purpose of the afternoon.

As often happens on such days you get lost in your thoughts and overwhelmed by the atmosphere of nature around you. I am a sucker for such indulgence and, not being able to locate any fresh rhino tracks, had wandered deep into my contented subconscious. It was only a couple of hours later, on my way back to the lodge, that I happened to glance out of the corner of my eye at a thick scaled tail in the nearby footwell. I nearly jumped out of my seat not expecting to see such a large snake there.

Only then did I remember the lizard!

The Flustered Farm Girl and her Fluffy Slipper Ranger
(Timbavati Private Nature Reserve, South Africa)

It's not just rough, tough, macho guides that encounter snakes. Game lodges and bush camps are built in prime reptile habitat. Also, snake prey such as rodents, lizards and amphibians, tend to make these areas their home. As a result, anyone who works in the game lodge industry has invariably had at least one snake experience. One particular camp manageress – an energetic and enthusiastic farm girl we'll call Liz – had two memorable encounters in quick succession.

At the beginning of winter one year, this particular young lady, finding the ladies' room occupied, darted into the unoccupied gents. The sense of urgency (or perhaps it was just the influence of alcohol) clouded her awareness a little, and, before she had really taken in her surroundings, she had her pants down and was experiencing some relief when she happened to glance down at her feet. A torpid adult Puff Adder lay flush with the bowl of the toilet. Liz leapt up – 'mid-wee' as she later described it – and dashed for the door only just managing to preserve her modesty before emerging in near hysteria in the midst of dinner.

A week later, this same manageress, early for dinner and having ensured that tables were laid properly and all staff were on duty, sat down on her favourite overstuffed couch to enjoy a gin and tonic before the guests arrived back from a game drive. Having savoured the first sip she sensed a presence at her shoulder and turned around expecting to see her partner. Instead she was greeted by a bright orange and black banded Eastern Tiger Snake that had emerged from between the couch cushions to investigate this disturbance of its early winter aestivation.

Needless to say the two experiences in such quick succession brought forth ample ribbing and Freudian innuendo over the ensuing months. Liz's partner, himself formerly a guide of some repute, and not someone to let such an opportunity pass by, was a regular contributor to said ribbing. It was not much later that winter, however, before the shoe (or in this case, the slipper) was on the other foot.

The home of this couple was situated beneath the canopy of a Broad-pod False-thorn on the banks of a seasonal watercourse a fair distance from the rest of the staff accommodation. Its isolation resulted in many thrilling nocturnal wildlife encounters and the farm girl and her beau got used to avoiding buffalo at night, hearing lions roaring in the river-bed during their slumbers and watching elephant from their deck on afternoons off. The two even managed a study of the breeding cycle of a pair of Violet-backed Starlings that mistakenly chose the security of a Tree Wisteria leaning against the deck in which to breed: Mistakenly because the breeding attempt failed due to the depredations of a boomslang.

Perhaps it was the thought of this boomslang that lingered in the subconscious of our hero as he awoke and absentmindedly slipped on his sheepskin slippers one morning. No sooner had he pushed his right foot into the comfort of the slipper than he leapt immediately backwards onto the bed, landing upright on his feet and stirring the bemused Liz. 'Get the broomstick!' he shouted, in an authoritative voice only slightly higher pitched than normal (it was early in the morning after all), 'I've been bitten by a snake.'

Dutifully, Liz rushed off to the other room, retrieved the broom and came back to find her source of strength and courage backed up against the headboard. Grabbing the broom and gesturing to her to move back into the doorway, he gingerly probed the slipper, expecting the immediate strike of whatever snake lay within. When this was not forthcoming he lifted the slipper up on the end of the broom and gently shook it to prise the occupant loose. Sure enough a small safety pin tumbled down and landed on the polished concrete floor. The audible, distinctly unreptilian tinkling caused this erstwhile Crocodile Dundee to instantly flush a shade of crimson through his deep tan.

Birding
(The Pursuit of Avian Gnosis)

by JAMES HENDRY

Bird – The Shorter Oxford English Dictionary, published in 1970, defines the verb 'bird' as 'to catch or shoot birds'.

Birder (or birdwatcher) – Someone interested in feathered fauna. Their interest may extend no further than throwing a few crumbs out for the village sparrows or might stretch to spending inordinate amounts of time and money in the endless quest for ornithological wisdom.

Field Guide – A book containing illustrations or photographs, distribution maps and snippets of information on the birds in a particular region.

Lifer – The first sighting of a particular species, the prospect of which may result in quivers of excitement and uncontrolled dribbling.

Life List – The total number of bird species that a birdwatcher has seen. The life list is a source of some pride for serious twitchers.

Tick – A member of one's life list.

Mega-Tick – An especially prized member of one's life list.

Twitcher – This is traditionally a birder who is interested more in accumulating new species for their life list than in bird biology. They have been known to spend absurd amounts of currency flying to far-flung corners of the globe for fleeting glimpses of rare and hitherto unobserved birds. The term is also used, more loosely, as a synonym for any keen birder.

Worldwide there are in excess of eighty million birders who are prepared to travel abroad annually, spending a quite fantastic $80 billion as they jet about the world for lifers. Southern Africa has a total species list of just under a thousand which is rather impressive for a region of its size. In a life-time of climbing briar-covered hills, crawling through smelly bogs, being savaged by Highland cleggs – all in the driving rain or sleet – British birders would consider themselves extremely lucky to tick more than four hundred species. The whole of Europe boasts a species list of just over nine hundred, while the vast expanse that is the US and Canada lays claim to just a few more. Yet southern African travel companies are still bent on marketing the banal 'Big Five' at the expense of attracting more of the moneyed twitchers who might come to southern Africa and see four hundred new birds in just over three weeks.

The first thing one needs, when learning to bird, is a pair of decent binoculars. These essential tools range in price from just over one hundred rand to well in excess of fifteen thousand. The pricey ones are certainly the best in the business but one does not need to spend the GDP of a small country to obtain a pair that is adequate for identifying birds. Next on the list is a good field guide. There are two main ones available in southern Africa and the vociferous arguments that ensue amongst loyal punters of each publication often result in fisticuffs. Having acquired the requisite equipment all that is required is a bird to peer at with your binoculars and identify with your field guide. Simple.

I developed an interest in birds only fairly late in life. As my years of nature guiding have progressed so my fascination with this spectacularly diverse group of vertebrates has intensified. Before leaving an unpromising career as the next Eric Clapton, I never considered that I might understand the rush that birders derive from spotting a new or rare bird. To my great surprise I now find myself crawling through rocky grassland for a glimpse of a tiny quail or wading through deep mud for a crake or rail which I can hear calling in the reeds. Indeed, the scratches and cuts from creeping through thorny, tangled riverine bush to identify a secretive bird's twittering call are some of the most rewarding I have inflicted on myself. I shall always derive solace from the instant calming serenity of looking up at the sky where a lone vulture soars between the clouds in the midday heat, so high it is but a tiny

BEE-EATERS

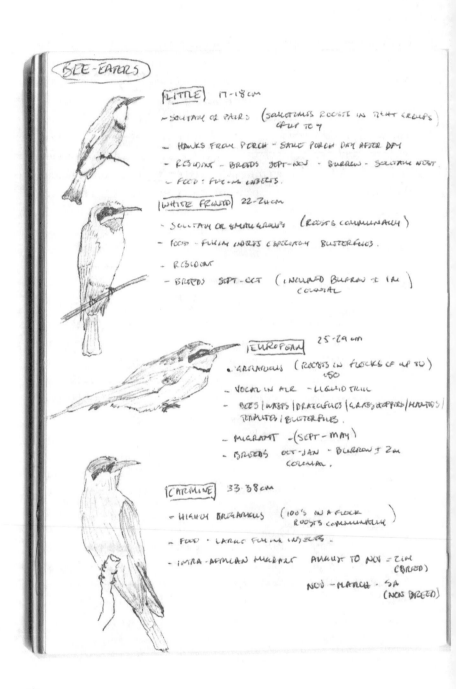

LITTLE 17-18 cm

- SOLITARY OR PAIRS (SOMETIMES ROOSTS IN TIGHT GROUPS OF UP TO 4)
- HAWKS FROM PERCH - SAME PERCH DAY AFTER DAY
- RESIDENT - BREEDS SEPT-NOV - BURROW - SOLITARY NEST
- FOOD: FLYING INSECTS.

WHITE FRONTED 22-24 cm

- SOLITARY OR SMALL GROUPS (ROOSTS COMMUNALLY)
- FOOD - FLYING INSECTS ESPECIALLY BUTTERFLIES.
- RESIDENT
- BREEDS SEPT-OCT (INCLINED BURROW ± 1M) COLONIAL

EUROPEAN 25-29 cm

- GREGARIOUS (ROOSTS IN FLOCKS OF UP TO) 150
- VOCAL IN AIR - LIQUID TRILL
- BEES / WASPS / DRAGONFLIES / GRASSHOPPERS / MANTIDS / TERMITES / BUTTERFLIES.
- MIGRANT - (SEPT - MAY)
- BREEDS OCT-JAN - BURROW ± 2M COLONIAL.

CARMINE 33-38 cm

- HIGHLY GREGARIOUS (100'S IN A FLOCK ROOSTS COMMUNALLY)
- FOOD - LARGE FLYING INSECTS.
- INTRA-AFRICAN MIGRANT — AUGUST TO NOV = ZIM (BREED)
  NOV - MARCH - SA (NON BREED)

WHITE CROWNED SHRIKE

SAT ON TOP MOST BARE
BRANCH OF TAMBOTI ABOVE
PILOTS HOUSE.

PREY: BIG FLYING INSECT
± 2 - 2½ CM

THE BIRD SHOOK INSECT AROUND, STOOD
ON IT AND PLUCKED ONE OF THE
WINGS OFF WHICH IT DISCARDED.
THE OTHER WING WAS EATEN.

FLIGHT VERY CHARACTERISTIC — SMALL WINGS?
SHALLOW WING BEATS.

FEEDING: A LONG PROCESS OF KILLING, CLEANING, + SWALLOWING
BILL CLEANED ON BRANCH AFTERWARDS.

RED CHESTED CUCKOO

BREEDING
MIGRANT: OCT - APRIL
(CENTRAL AFRICA)

CALLS ESPECIALLY AFTER RAIN
EVEN AT NIGHT

HOSTS: ROBINS / CHATS / THRUSHES
DUSKY FLYCATCHER
CAPE WAGTAIL
(1 EGG PER HOST NEST)

FOOD: INSECTS
ESPECIALLY CATERPILLARS.

CHICK EVICTS HOST EGGS AND/OR YOUNG
WITHIN 4 DAYS OF HATCHING.

fleck. This is a story of some of my birding experiences and how they have fuelled my love for things natural.

Once Bitten

My first experience was not promising. I was five years old and the family was taking its first trip to the world-famous Kruger National Park (KNP). After a six-hour trip of car sickness, I was sent off to go birdwatching with some older kids who were none too pleased to be saddled with a small vomit bag. I thought it all quite exciting to start with. I was instructed to lie down under a low bush while one of the others leopard-crawled across the camp lawn to sprinkle stale breadcrumbs in front of our make-shift hide. After what seemed like an age, a small, dull, brownish bird descended from a nearby shrub to choruses of 'Ooh, it's a Southern Grey-headed Sparrow!' I thought waiting in the forty degree heat for such obscurity a complete waste of time . . .

As a student, I conducted a survey amongst the Zulu people of the oNgoye Forest. I was wandering through the forest one day with a vastly more knowledgeable student when he froze. I thought he must have spotted a forest bandit. His face had gone quite white and he began to stutter. Anxious that he was having some sort of pulmonary attack, I tapped him on the shoulder. He turned his head slowly to one side and urgently motioned for me to shut up.

'Delegorgue's Pigeons!' he hissed, staring intently into the nearby trees.

I peered blankly into the various shades of green and brown, seeing nothing. He handed me his binoculars and I beheld two brown things that looked rather like the Rock Doves of which I had seen thousands in Johannesburg. I handed the binoculars back to my enthralled companion, emulating his look of dumbfounded amazement so as not to betray my ignorance. This bird (now rather unromantically called the Eastern Bronze-naped Pigeon) is quite a localised species and we were, in fact, lucky to see it.

After my degree, I was at a loss as to what to do. Somehow I ended up on a ranger training course not far from where my Zoology field trips had been conducted. This was when I had to face the fact that learning to identify birds was going to have to become a priority if I was to make a success of being a guide.

The Lark and the Kingfisher

When I arrived at the training course I was in possession of a pair of binoculars that predated the First World War. Although I am sure they were useful for spotting the Red Baron as he puttered out from the horizon, they were not a great help to me as I tried to fathom the intimidating avian diversity of Maputaland. I was, by some margin, the most incompetent birder on the course. The thing with birds is that they seldom sit still long enough for one to have a good look at them. Trees were far easier. If I could not figure out what they were, I could always go back there the next day and they would still be there. I could lift their branches, feel the texture of their bark, pick their leaves and smell their flowers. Birds were a different story. Just as I managed to focus my ancient pair of field glasses on them, they would fly off or hide behind a leaf.

Then there was one sighting that probably sealed my lasting interest in ornithology.

It was early one morning and I was drinking a cup of evil-tasting coffee, overlooking the floodplain below the training camp. Two juvenile Martial Eagles (Africa's largest eagles) swooped down overhead, tucked back their wings and scorched down into the floodplain. Flying parallel with the plain-bank, they used the topography perfectly to conceal their approach from a small nursery herd of impala feeding on the lip of the plain. Just as they reached the foot of the hill they levelled and simultaneously ripped their talons into an unsuspecting little lamb. I was astonished at their speed, stealth and skill.

The rest of the course was spent playing catch-up with the other trainees – who seemed able to identify the tiniest birds from half-second glimpses. 'Ah yes, that was a Striped Kingfisher,' one of them would chime as a tiny, indistinct bird afforded a fleeting hint as it perched in impenetrable foliage a hundred metres away.

'How in the name of roast chicken is it possible to identify a bird no bigger than a cigarette box as it scoots past doing Mach III?' I would ask, in exasperation.

'Simple really, did you not see the whitish body and striped head, with a slight blue tinge on the back as it flew? Or perhaps the way it flew vertically up to its perch,' said Isobel, our trainer.

'No,' I said, 'All I saw was a minute speck speeding past so fast that it may as well have been a hypersonic mosquito.'

She looked a little disappointed but said that I might, perhaps, after a long time, begin to understand this birding thing. Soon after that we were heading out to find some rhino tracks, when a little brown bird settled on a log in front of the vehicle. It began to sing loudly and melodiously. Isobel turned to me and asked, 'Well, James, why don't you try to identify this one?'

'Ah, a Rufous-Naped Lark,' said I, quick as a flash.

Her jaw hung agape and my peers stared goggled-eyed as I tried to look complacent.

Isobel enquired how I had managed to come to such a speedy and uncharacteristically correct conclusion. I shrugged my shoulders and mumbled something about practising a bit. In actual fact it was pot-luck. This particular lark was the only one I could remember from the seemingly endless number of indistinguishable little brown tweeters in my field guide. I happened to remember a folk song mentioning singing larks and took a flyer at the only lark I knew. The same day another trainee managed to spot a Rudd's Apalis which, I was told, was an outstanding tick to have. Oh, goody, I thought, I will be able to tell other naturalists that I have seen it and impress them even if I wouldn't be able to identify it again should it fly into my face.

After training I was dispatched to a private reserve in the central KNP. The camp was situated in the midst of Mopane Woodland. The woodland is rather mono-specific as far as trees go but the mopane tree is a special one. Amongst other things, it is host to a bracket fungus that eats away at the heartwood creating unrivalled nesting opportunities for birds that like to nest in tree holes; hornbills, starlings, hoopoes and woodpeckers to name a few. But the hole-nesting bird which made the greatest impression on me is also the bird whose call I first learnt to recognise and I must dedicate a brief digression to him.

In the early spring, fat and inspired, he leaves his wintering grounds south of the Sahara. He is bound for southern Africa, flushed with insatiable excitement at the thought of breeding prospects. Like an F15 at full throttle he zooms south, trying to out-fly potential mating competitors. He is a handsome fellow with a pearly white front, a two-toned red and black beak and a black mask that makes him look a little like a flying pirate. His stunning azure-turquoise back glints as he banks to the rising sun. He is, of course, the Woodland Kingfisher and apart from being rather fetching he is, by some margin, the most vociferous bird in the region. Although a kingfisher, he does not eat fish but prefers invertebrates and small reptiles. The mopane is full of both of these and doubly suitable because he and his wife like to nest in tree holes.

His call is an easily distinguished and strident 'chip prrrrrrrrrrrrr'. If he did this once in a while it might be quite appealing but he screeches from first light to just after dark and sometimes at midnight. The greater the density of the little blighters, the louder and more frequently they feel it necessary to yell at each other. By the end of the summer I could not wait for them to head back north, hoping that they might forget to stop before the Sahara and become lost somewhere in Libya where Ghaddafi could use them for missile practice. This bird's breeding antics are mirthful. When a male finds a mate they hop on to an exposed twig, hold their wings out and then pirouette around and around, chirring like demented alarm clocks. What is most amazing about this species is that its entire breeding cycle, from egg laying to fledging takes less than six weeks and yet he must yell his pharynx off for the best part of five months.

Hiding from the Olive Woodpecker

Once qualified as a guide, I could no longer simply ignore the birds I was not sure of. I had to justify to my guests why one particularly nondescript pipit was not the same as another slightly different, equally nondescript pipit. My birding knowledge was still scanty, but I worked at it. Once I had developed a better than average understanding of the reserve's bird list, it added immeasurably to the game drives and walks I took as I was able to fill mammal-free gaps with birding snippets. Sometimes I even tweaked an interest in guests that they never knew existed.

There are various deplorable techniques employed by not-great guides which I have to admit I used at the beginning of my career. On sighting an enormous brown eagle-type thing perching conspicuously in a dead tree, I would drop my head to the right, accelerate, and study the road next to the driver's seat with great concentration. 'Ooh's and 'aah's from behind me were ignored until I was sure the bird was out of sight. I would then look up and say something like, 'Gee, fresh leopard tracks!' or 'Did you see something?'

But as my confidence grew, I was happy to tell guests that I did not know which bird it was exactly. I would identify it for them with the aid of the bird guide, thus augmenting my skill as a birder.

Guests who claim to enjoy birds come in a number of categories. Their binoculars are the first clue. If they have none, I know that perhaps they put the odd papaya out for the birds at home after breakfast and that is the extent of it. They are often extremely interested novices who will stop me for every brown feather they see and then fight over my binoculars and field guide to identify it first. It is such a pleasure to see people's interest shift from lions to larks over the space of a weekend.

A pair of spanking new, 'his and hers', unscathed and pricey Swarovski binoculars often means: 'The Joneses have started birding and thus we have too. We know all the authors of southern African field guides on first name basis, and ornithology is lucky to have us'. The Swarovskis are trained on all flying things (including wasps and butterflies) and then a race for quickest identification ensues. If all concur with the identification, a smug smile develops on the successful spotter's face. If the classification is incorrect, however, numerous reasons are advanced for the mistake . . . 'There appears to be a smudge on my lens,' or 'that must have been juvenile plumage . . .'

One such ornithological mastermind had brought his new belle out to the bush for a weekend. All weekend he regaled the poor girl with tales of his hunting prowess and spouted every hackneyed and nonsensical bush legend available. As a flock of Green Wood-Hoopoes flew overhead, he informed me that he regularly saw the similar Violet Wood-Hoopoe in his Johannesburg garden. This was too good an opportunity to pass up. I opened my field guide, smiled, and pointed to the distribution map for the Violet Wood-Hoopoe which indicated that this rather uncommon bird is only found in Namibia. I suggested that it was perhaps the same Green Wood-Hoopoe we had just seen that visited his garden. He eyed me with utter contempt and reasserted that he could not possibly have been mistaken. Ah yes, the only Violet Wood-Hoopoe to ever cross the Kalahari Desert must have slipped into Johannesburg, unnoticed by the countless hundreds of fanatical twitchers that live between there and Windhoek, and plopped safely down into your garden. A little later we were speeding for the lodge, late for an airplane when he said, 'Pass me your field guide.'

I tossed him the book and drove on. A second later he proclaimed, 'Yes, I just saw an Olive Woodpecker.'

'You mean the Olive Woodpecker that only occurs in montane or coastal forest, the one whose distribution does not include this area,' said I, '*that* Olive Woodpecker?'

'Yes, of course,' he scowled.

'Right, I will contact the Bird Atlas people immediately we return and inform them that we have a first record for the area.'

The genuinely interested and experienced birders often have a well-worn pair of good binoculars and a scuffed old bird guide. They are such a pleasure to guide. Partly because I learn a lot from them, partly because they love being in wild places and are fascinated by so many aspects of ecology. I have spent countless pleasurable hours on game drives and walks, discussing birds with enthralled birders. Time melts away when faced with identifying flycatchers, cisticolas, soaring specks and warbling calls. There is nothing quite so peaceful as immersing oneself in the morning bird song trying to discern the individuals from the chorus.

Heralds of the spring

The return of other birds was a far more pleasant occurrence than the return of the noisy little kingfisher. After a dry and chilly winter, the first sighting of a thin-tailed Wahlberg's Eagle in late August was an eagerly sought herald of winter's end. These remarkable eagles pair for life and return to the same nesting sites year after year. On the reserve where I worked, there was one couple I had a particular soft spot for. The male was a less common pale form, with a snowy white front, black eyes and brown wings. His wife was a dark chocolate brown and their home was (and probably still is) in a Knob Thorn tree on the banks of a shady drainage line surrounded by lush Tamboti and Jackal-berry trees and, in September, blinding red swathes of Weeping Boer-bean flowers. Every August I would eagerly await a first sighting of him, perched imperiously atop a dead Leadwood tree near his nest, absorbing the morning sun.

A bit later the other heralds of the summer would arrive: Barn Swallows and Willow Warblers from the UK and Europe. How on earth these tiny things, with brains barely bigger than almonds, are able to find their way here all the way from the Palaearctic is quite astounding. Apparently migrants process all sorts of environmental cues such as the sun, the stars, the earth's magnetism, smells, noises, prevailing winds, landscape features and combinations of all these. Other migrants like European and Southern Carmine Bee-eaters, cuckoos, Violet-backed Starlings and the Steppe Eagles (all the way from Siberia) all make the effort to put in a summer appearance in the lowveld. Some come to breed and others to fatten up and rest after exhausting mating efforts north of the equator.

Breeding Folly

Apart from my friend the Woodland Kingfisher, there are a number of birds worldwide who have elaborate and seemingly pointless mating habits. Bower birds from New Guinea and Australia build complicated little houses of sticks and leaves that serve no purpose other than to attract mates; they are not even used for nesting. Back home the Red-crested Korhaan must have the most bizarre territorial and mating antics. He is not particularly aerodynamic and resembles a baby ostrich. His territorial activities have earned him the name 'Suicide Bird'.

'Click . . . click . . . click . . . click,' he begins, snapping his beak loudly. On the last snap he starts to utter a woeful, ascending tooting with his beak pointed heavenward. This is to attract the attentions of all the other korhaans in the area. Once he is sure they are all watching, he takes off, flapping his wings with huge effort, rising sharply above the tree-line before stalling and then plummeting to the ground, just remembering to open his wings before crashing down. If it is mating season and this display is suitably impressive, he may attract the attentions of a female. Once she is in his sights he begins an intricate dance. With his head tucked as far into his shoulders as his long neck will allow, he stiffens every muscle in his body. Thus set, he begins a slow 'Riverdance' style ballet. Sometime during this absurd cabaret he erects the red crest which gives him his name. By the time he reaches the climax of his performance, she has lost interest and wandered off to find a spider or grub to nibble on. He looks hurt, folds his crest and Riverdances over to her whereupon he re-erects his plume. This pantomime continues until she eventually relents.

RED CRESTED KORHAAN

RED CREST
PARTIALLY
ERECTED

RED CREST
FULLY
BEHIND

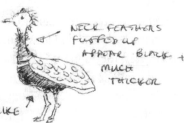

NECK FEATHERS
FUFFED UP
APPEAR BLACK +
MUCH
THICKER

♂ HOPPED AFTER ♀ LOOKING LIKE

♀ WALKED HURRIEDLY OFF

♂ STOPPED + CLICKED TONGUE 4-6 TIMES WITH CORRESPONDING NECK ACTION

THIN PROCESS REPEATED - MALE HOPS ABOUT 4-5 TIMES AFTER FEMALE FEMALE RUNS OFF MALES CLICKS TONGUE (CLACKS BEAK?) THEN HOPS OFF AFTER HER AGAIN

NB NO SUICIDE FLIGHT (TERRITORIAL/AGGRESSION ONLY?)

⌈ BIG DAM ROAD ⌉
│ 19/10/97 │
⌊ ± 5.40 PM ⌋

120

Then there are the parasitic cuckoos that lay their eggs in other birds' nests and play no further parental role. This rather inconsiderate habit is made worse by the fact that cuckoo chicks are wont to either push their step-siblings from the nest or simply peck them to death as soon as they hatch. The Levaillant's Cuckoo's preferred host is the Arrow-marked Babbler. The babbler flocks recognise the adult cuckoos for the insidious things they are but once the cuckoo chick arrives, they will raise it as their own. Almost all southern African cuckoos migrate away from the region for the winter but the odd Levaillant's Cuckoo, in its first year, has been known to hang around with its adoptive babbler family for the colder months. The cuckoo soon begins to resemble its biological parents yet the babblers at no stage associate it with the adults they violently harried away at the beginning of the breeding season. I have been most amused watching a Levaillant's Cuckoo, spending his first winter here, flitting about with his family of babblers. I am sure it is most confusing for him being far larger and a completely different colour from them. He does make vague attempts to fit in by imitating their calls in tone-deaf fashion.

Songs of Love and War

Birds like to sing because they are territorial or because, like rock stars, they think their songs will be attractive to potential mates. Francolins are different, they also screech in order to terrify the wits out of predators (and people) who happen to be walking past. Walking along one peaceful afternoon a trainee and I were talking about rhino behaviour. We were approaching a large waterhole and I explained that rhino often like to rest in the mud on hot afternoons. Silence ensued as we neared the muddy pans at the northern end of the water. We treaded as lightly and slowly as possible, peering through the gaps in the foliage. The only sound was that of our breathing.

'BLEEH BLEEH BLEH BLEH!' screeched four Natal Francolins as they exploded out from under our feet. My companion (who had been a soldier) swore violently, flung his rifle to his shoulder and simultaneously dived for cover expecting to defend us from a terrorist ambush. The fowl settled a little way off to laugh at their trick.

The dawn chorus is rather dull of a winter's morning, probably because most birds are too cold to talk. I know I am. I have spent many a morning driving out before the sun wakes, blabbering incoherent nonsense at my guests because my jaw and tongue are frigid. At this time Red-billed Hornbills perch high in dead trees. They face east, white breast feathers puffed to the maximum, glaring unmoving at passers-by. They sit completely still, not wanting to upset the thin layer of surrounding warmth they have created in the still air. The francolins, who love any excuse to make a huge cacophony, are not fazed by the cold as they squawk merrily away at each other.

In the spring the harmonies are inspiring. Again it is normally the francolins who wake everyone (bar the odd irritatingly enthusiastic Woodland Kingfisher.) After that there is an oratorio of unnumbered voices. Crested Barbets churr, Bearded Woodpeckers drum, Blue Waxbills whistle the wispy high notes, White-browed Scrub-Robins blow the mid-register and Southern Ground-Hornbills toot the bass. Greyheaded Bush-Shrikes resonate in the background, Eastern Black-headed Orioles intersperse with crystal chant whilst the Dark-capped Bulbuls, babblers and Yellow-billed Hornbills sing the chorus and the Sabota Lark belts out the descant.

Songs, displays, ticks, lifers and birders; all have giveen me the greatest pleasure. There are birds everywhere from the Arctic to the Antarctic and seldom a time when an avian interest cannot be satisfied. There are even Peregrine Falcons in New York City (or Cape Town). I suspect one of the reasons they have lasted so long there is that they give people a tenuous connection with the wild. Be it in a desert, a forest or on the coast, birds are a fascinating way to enjoy the fullness of nature. After all, eighty million people can't be wrong!

The Whites of Their Eyes

Nocturnal felines like lion and leopard have white markings beneath their eyes, while diurnal species such as cheetah do not. These white markings are commonly believed to enhance their nocturnal vision by reflecting more light into their eyes.

Yet our eyes detect shapes by the light reflected off the objects we are looking at. Light from another source usually affects our nocturnal vision negatively – like a light in the distance. A study of the markings beneath cats' eyes also brings into question how much light is actually reflected into their pupils. Perhaps there is another reason.

One possibility may be that they are used for communication. Because vocal communication is relatively limited in animals, 'body language' plays a crucial role in communication between individuals of the same species (and to a lesser degree between different species). Posturing, lateral displays, tail and head positions and aggressive displays are just a few ways in which animals send physical messages to one another. These are all very visual signals and therefore less obvious after dark. However, contrasting facial markings such as the white patches beneath the eyes of genets, the white line between the eyes – or chevron – of the kudu, the lighter rings around many of the smaller antelopes eyes and the white muzzles of many antelope and carnivores make the position of the animal's head and therefore its posture easier to detect. Likewise, the bold stripes and/or spots on the sides of kudu, nyala and bushbuck and the white markings on their dorsal crests are probably not much use as camouflage but at close range make a lateral display in thick bush easy to detect for these animals for whom such posturing plays an important social function. Perhaps the subtle light markings beneath the eyes of cats (from the mighty tiger to the tiny Small-spotted Cat) serve more effectively as an intraspecific communicative device than a vision-enhancing tool.

While we are on the topic there is another myth that needs addressing. It is sometimes said that gemsbok use the black and white stripes on their face to enhance their vision. They look down the black, light-absorbing stripe during the day and down the white, reflective stripe at night. It's a nice idea but the same doubts arise, besides which, surely the poor animal would prefer not to have to squint for such long periods!

David Hood

Things that Go *Bump* in the Night

(Burglars in the Bush)

by MEGAN EMMETT

s a rule, rangers sleep soundly. It's not a common thing to encounter a ranger that has any trouble sleeping – I certainly don't think I have met such a person. The early mornings and late nights, combined with the sometimes-excessive heat of the bushveld, generally ensure that by bedtime I'm literally 'bushed'. That, in combination with the chirr of a cricket orchestra, the 'Good-Lord-deliver-us' chant of the Fiery-necked Nightjar and the distant roar of a lion, is like a drug. Sleep generally arrives in the eyelid region before contact is even made with the pillow. Personally, even before becoming a ranger, I have always had extraordinary sleeping abilities, lulled almost instantly into head-lolling slumber every time I get into a car to make a long-distance (or even not so long-distance) journey.

So it was that I was *fast* asleep when the proverbial 'bump' in the night clambered through my door. The bump's name was Brent and, at an easy six feet tall, he was certainly a disturbance, bashing around noisily in the pitch darkness. In a state of sleepy disorientation, I somehow sensed the urgency of his movements and lifted my head from its blissful spot on the pillow.

'What Brent?' I mumbled, a little confused as to why he was standing in the middle of my room in the middle of the night, bumping around while I was trying to sleep. 'What do you want?'

'Meg . . . Meg . . . quick . . . the keys!' came the frantic plea, 'I need the safe keys, where are they?'

Now, in the light of the fact that there was only a single set of keys for the rifle safe at this safari camp and that I had used them last to lock away my .375 rifle after a game drive, it shouldn't seem strange that Brent had come to request them of me. That's how it always worked. Whoever had them last, kept them and, when required, the other ranger would just seek them out. However, what *was* troubling was why Brent wanted these keys at one o'clock in the morning.

'What?' was all I could manage. My brain just could not understand what this lunatic was doing disturbing my precious sleep, or why he had not chosen to turn on the light, to see for himself where the keys were, if he needed them so urgently.

'What for?' I tried again.

'There are burglars in the kitchen,' came the *very* unexpected response.

I clawed at the bedside light, illuminating the room with an even more disorientating stimulus. Somehow, with the word 'burglar', my brain had made the association and injected a hefty dose of adrenalin into my system. I was now awake.

'There, on the desk,' I said, pointing to the table opposite my bed. Brent grabbed the keys from the table and darted out of the room, whispering a stern 'Stay here!' over his shoulder.

Disobeying immediately, I dashed from my bed, throwing yesterday's khaki shirt over my sleepwear as I bolted out of the door after him. I was met outside by the camp manageress, Kate, who had been woken by one of the two security guards. These security guards were of course armed with torches and not weapons as their job was to detect and keep animals – and not criminals – at bay. As a general rule, the former is far more of a danger in the wilds of Africa. Naturally the guard's first stop on detecting the uninvited visitors in the kitchen (a glance through the window to investigate the racket had confirmed them to be burglars and not marauding Honey Badgers) was Brent-the-ranger's room. A garbled explanation to a sleepy, dishevelled Brent had bolted him from his own deep ranger sleep. Immediately he began strategizing a capture plan with the guards and the now-also-awoken tracker, Abednigo, a Shangane giant and a useful ally in any dodgy situation.

Left standing bewildered in the dark, not really sure how to help (calling the police was a futile exercise, they were an hour's drive away and probably would not have responded until morning anyway) Kate and I garbled excited 'Oh my goodness's and 'I hope no-one gets hurt's to one another, adrenalin still tingling in our bodies from the surprise of the initial news.

'They're stealing the cutlery and the champagne,' Kate sighed, and then, as it dawned on her, she added, 'they must just touch my muffins for morning game drive and I'll . . .' She let her voice trail off as her cheeks began to redden with anger.

We waited for what seemed like hours in the darkness, but in reality it was only a relatively short while before the guards and Brent, now beaming like a contented Cheshire cat, came marching around the corner with their unimpressed captives, their hands bound behind their backs with rope. Hardened criminals they were not. Poor youths with a propensity for mischief was probably more like it.

South African game reserves are often surrounded by communities that traditionally inhabited the land where the wildlife and tourists now roam. In the past, villagers and other people living within the area designated as a new reserve were sometimes forcibly removed with very little compensation for the loss of their land. Although relationships between these communities and the reserves are improving, jobs are still a problem. While private and government reserves have created a significant number of new posts, unemployment rates of up to eighty per cent are not uncommon. A network of extended family often results in one working person supporting ten. In these conditions petty crime easily becomes a way of life, although usually this assumes the form of subsistence poaching.

In our case, these juvenile delinquents braved the hazards of walking through the bush at night to perform a different form of poaching . . . that of Kate's home-baked muffins and a fridge full of long-life cream and Moët & Chandon.

One can't help but feel sorry for such villains. At the time I'd have loved to have made them both a sandwich and sent them home, cream in hand. Brent certainly had not needed his rifle or military strategy.

Kate, however, was not accessing her sense of compassion. She was ready to wield Brent's rifle herself on discovering that her morning-drive muffins had in fact been destroyed in the thieves' rushed packing job.

Muffins, poverty, bravery (or is walking through lion hunting grounds at night merely stupidity?), the law is the law and, as with any crime, the police had to be involved and the youths' erroneous ways corrected. This task of rehabilitation however, was one that Abednigo and the two security guards assumed responsibility for themselves.

Since the police confirmed our suspicions of only being able to respond to our robbery at first light, the guards and Abednigo detained the men in the tool shed where they set about chastising their subjects with statements such as: 'It's guys like you that give South Africa a bad name' and: 'You're young, don't ruin your chances by becoming a criminal'.

With the situation under control, my chief concern was resuming where I'd left off with the pillow. I headed straight back to my bed, intent on getting as many winks in before first light and the thud-clickity-click of my alarm clock due at five-thirty.

Dragging my carcass from the bed at five-thirty was never as easy as putting it there in the first place. And, after the antics of the early hours, it took every ounce of willpower to dress and head down to morning tea with the guests.

Later on that morning, I passed the tool shed on my way to retrieve the safe keys from Brent, to fetch my rifle for the morning game drive. Abednigo was still chinwagging with his prisoners and reluctant to forsake his post for his normal function of tracker.

Grateful that our morning would be spent searching for game and enjoying the sounds and crispness of the early part of the day, we left the thieves, still held captive in the tool shed, to Kate, who would hand them over to the police. Quite remarkably, when we stopped for coffee, our basket revealed a bundle of fresh, hot muffins. I stared at them as if they were a rare animal find. The guests eyed me suspiciously, unaware of the extraordinary events of the night.

I questioned Kate over breakfast, but her mind was occupied with another matter completely.

'You'll never guess it,' she exclaimed excitedly, ignoring my enquiries, 'those muffin thieves asked me for a job.'

'No ways,' interjected Brent, 'really?'

'Really!' Kate responded. 'Before the police arrived they begged me to hire them.'

'I can't believe the cheek!' I added, 'what job did they want?'

Kate looked up at me and her lips curled in amusement, 'They want to be security guards!'

Crutches and Lions

Mike, the camp manager, stepped out from his house, freshly spruced for dinner, the plaster cast on his broken ankle polished, his crutches glinting in the starlight. Used to the crutches, he deftly lifted himself from his deck and onto the path. As you can imagine, shining a torch with any degree of efficiency while propelling oneself on crutches is not possible. He did not see the small group of buffalo on his left. He did not see the lions on his right. The lions saw the buffalo.

There is that briefest of moments when one knows something is wrong but cannot figure out what it is. This was the moment that the lions chose to make their move. Lions charged buffalo, buffalo counter-charged. The cats growled and snarled while their quarry bellowed. Dust clouds choked the air. Mike, meanwhile, performed a feat of athleticism seldom seen outside of championship track and field. Fuelled by a massive adrenalin surge, he reversed on his crutches without his feet touching the ground. Two spectacular pole vaults and a long jump later he was back on his deck.

James Hendry

The Puff Adder and the Hyeana

(Somewhere in the Mopane, Northern Botswana)

by DAVID HOOD

The heat was not oppressive, but it surrounded you, holding you in its undeniable grip. It asserted itself without presumption.

In the camp, sandy walkways linked the spacious safari tents and the lodge building, which together formed a big arc on the edge of a patch of riparian forest. These structures overlooked one of the Okavango Delta's large floodplains. The walkways were raked meticulously every morning and in places the lush vegetation had to be cut back to keep the paths clear.

I was looking after the camp while the managers were away on their leave and there was a lot to do that day. In order to get it all done I was hurrying along one of these sandy pathways, close to the lodge, when something stopped me dead.

Tracks!

Across the neatly raked pathway a patch about six or seven centimetres wide and spanning the path had been smoothed down. I knelt down

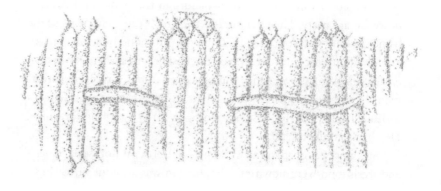

to inspect it. Across the breadth of the smoothed section was a series of small lines. They were clearly visible in places where the sand was particularly fine. The lines were evenly spaced, not quite reaching either edge. After a brief study I recognised them as the belly scales of a snake. The shape of the track indicated that the snake had been moving in a straight line. Only two snakes in Botswana are capable of moving with rectilinear motion as this one had done. They are the Puff Adder and the Southern African Python. Other snakes move with either a serpentine motion, leaving a zigzag track, or, more rarely, with a sidewinding motion, leaving a series of lines.

The broad, closely spaced belly scales of this track indicated that it had been made by a Puff Adder. Along the centre of the track there were irregular shallow scrape marks. The Puff Adder is a fat, short-tailed snake and, as a result, it drags only the tip of its tail in the sand behind it. The width of the smoothed down area indicated that this was a rather large specimen.

I had seen a Puff Adder track of similar size near the lodge a few days before. This was the second time, indicating that the snake had probably been spending time in the area. Snakes were fine, snakes were OK, and I was OK with snakes: We regularly saw Black Mambas and Mozambique Spitting Cobras in the camp, and I considered it acceptable as long as they didn't take up residence in the lodge or in one of the guest tents. They were welcome to visit *briefly*! I had no problem with picking up and moving certain snakes, provided they did not have a skull and crossbones next to their picture in the book. Puff Adders, however, are nasty. Their venom is cytotoxic, it causes necrosis of the tissue it comes into contact with. Our bodies respond by sending masses of fluid into the infected limb often causing it to swell to more than double its original size. Once this process is under way, even if treatment is given immediately, permanent scarring can be considered a fortunate outcome, the loss of a limb, or part thereof, unfortunate. Death, also unfortunate.

Our camp was deep in the wilderness of northern Botswana. Guests and fresh food were flown in. The drive in was arduous, involving a lot of sandy four-by-four driving, difficult water crossings and if it rained . . . If it rained, the fun really started. One mistake could turn a day's journey into a two or three day digging-and-pushing adventure.

Because of our isolated situation, I was acutely aware of the difficulties involved in getting a patient to a doctor quickly. Immediate medical help here involved a small green case that looked like a soap dish and was called 'Aspivenin'. Inside it had a plastic implement that looked like a syringe with a number of different attachments. You had to put one of the small cup-shaped attachments on the end of the syringe, place it over the bite and pump the syringe, creating suction. I valued this piece of equipment highly, but kept in mind that it was only a modern version of the old remedy that prescribed the laceration of the area around the wound before sucking out as much of the venom as you could. It was certainly far from foolproof.

And then there were the adrenaline and antihistamine injections, which were another reason I did not want that snake around. However good it feels to be a hero, I'd rather not have to use injections to become one. In northern Botswana there is a VHF channel used for emergencies only. If you pick up the handset and call into it at any time of day or night, a very calm voice answers on the other side and asks in a slightly disinterested manner how they can help. After you have managed to say that there is a person dying of malaria outside the door, or have described a severe injury using the gaps between screams to transmit clearly, the voice proceeds to come up with something you would never have thought of. I remember just such an incidence.

The lodge barman had been fishing with some of the staff on a quiet day at the camp. Whilst the group was dragging a net across a shallow pond, one of their number had felt something brush his leg. He had assumed it was a large fish known as a barbel. When the barman started to scream his companions laughed, thinking that he had also felt the fish and had got a fright. When a crocodile close to four metres in length had shown itself, the waiter who was closest, kicked it.

The crocodile let go; quite possibly it had felt trapped rather than hungry. I am not sure it would have let go if it had been looking for a meal. The guide who was with them was initially unable to drive, shaken by the experience, but after some urgent coercion, he gathered himself and brought the victim back to camp.

After the injuries had been described on the emergency channel, the voice on the other end had asked: 'Have you got Milton's drain cleaner, the blue bottle?'

'Affirmative.'

'Rinse the wound with that for at least twenty minutes.'

'. . . copy that.'

Despite the barman being in hospital and on antibiotics for a further month, the verdict was that Milton's drain cleaner had saved his leg.

Nevertheless, the stuff we had in the metal first-aid boxes was dangerous. In my mind horrific scenarios began to play out:

'Confirm you have adrenalin in one-ampoule bottles?'

'Affirmative.'

'Good, break the neck of the bottle and pour it into a syringe.'

'OK, what now?'

'Have you got a big needle?'

'Affirmative.'

'Have you seen the Quentin Tarantino film *Pulp Fiction*?'

The mind plays tricks, but my mind was made up. I had seen how unobservant guests could be in an environment so unfamiliar to them. Add to this the fact that Puff Adders are 'lazy' snakes and account for the largest percentage of bites in southern Africa simply because they don't bother to move until you step on them . . . a recipe for disaster!

Sadly the Puff Adder failed to heed my telepathic warning and was discovered a few days later lying motionless in leaf litter outside the kitchen door. It really was quite large and turned out to be just short of a metre long. It was beautiful too and I regretted not having a snake capture team at my disposal. I however, was not going to take any chances.

By the time I arrived a fascinated crowd, some on the verge of hysteria, had surrounded the snake. These onlookers were placated slightly by the sight of the .22 air rifle in my hands and began to relax further when, after a few dull thuds from the rifle, I carried the snake off to reside temporarily behind my desk.

The camp managers returned from leave a day later, much to my relief – the lives of the guests out here in this savage wilderness now felt somehow less my responsibility. The Puff Adder, meanwhile, was becoming more my responsibility as a certain stench had begun to emanate from my corner of the office. Despite this, I was determined that the life I had taken should not be in vain and refused to throw it out.

To this seemingly noble end I begged the loan of a large glass salad bowl from Michelle, the manageress. She generously granted my wish and the bowl was immediately filled with vodka. This was the best substitute for formaldehyde that we could find. The bowl was to be the Puff Adder's new home. Across the top of the bowl, preventing excessive evaporation, was glued a large piece of white paper with information regarding its inhabitant inscribed neatly in my best handwriting.

The salad bowl was placed in the camp's small reed-walled museum alongside various skulls, pinned insects, pressed flowers and mean-looking arthropods in jam jars of Smirnoff. An active termite colony occupied a neatly fenced-off patch on the museum's earth floor. They had been there first and I had confined their movements slightly with a border of hardwood planks.

After rearranging the specimens to make place for the Puff Adder, I gazed out through the window, a square hole cut in the reeds. Beyond the museum, the ground sloped almost imperceptibly downward to meet the reedbeds of the nearby floodplain. Small islands dominated by the drooping fronds of Wild Date Palms rose out of a sea of dry reeds. On the far side of the floodplain, a spit of land separated this from the next floodplain. The raised ground provided a substrate for larger trees, which formed a green leafy curtain from this perspective. I often wondered at the fact that although I had only been working in Botswana for a year, it felt more like home than anywhere else I had been.

I fed the termites some sticks to prevent them eating the museum and left through the doorway, reminding myself to find a door for it at some stage.

So concluded the Puff Adder's last days and it was all but forgotten as life continued.

It must have been some weeks later when a strange thing happened at our little camp. It was late in the evening and the guests had already gone to bed after dinner. I had retired to my little reed-walled abode, but Darren, the manager and Michelle, his wife were finishing up in the office when they heard a strange noise. They went to investigate. It turned out to be a hyaena in the swimming pool. In fact, by the time they found it, it was a very tired hyaena.

The swimming pool had no steps, only a stainless-steel ladder, something millions of years of evolution had not equipped the hyaena to deal with. It was trapped, unable to clamber out over the pool's low rim. Lesser mortals may have left this 'ghastly' creature to its demise, particularly since one of its kind had recently stolen a Persian rug from the lodge, but Darren and Michelle began the rescue mission immediately.

Darren slid one of the pool loungers into the water as a ramp for the hyaena to clamber onto. The exhausted creature didn't see it as such and swam away to the other side. No amount of herding could convince it to use this escape route. The added effort on the hyaena's part was taking its toll and it was clear it was not going to last much longer.

At last, as the hyaena swam away from one of Darren's desperate efforts, it came close to the edge and Michelle, fearing for its life, grabbed it by the scruff of its neck and hauled it onto the wooden deck. The hyaena did not struggle, but once it was out, regained its feet and stood looking at the two managers for some time.

Just looking. It may have just been tired and bewildered and uncertain of what to do next. I doubt it. Perhaps it was acknowledging the humans that had saved its life.

After a while it turned and walked off into the night.

The question that arose was: Why did the hyaena fall into the swimming pool? Yes, hippo have been known to become trapped in swimming pools, but they are amphibious creatures. It's easy to understand the association of a swimming pool with a little pond in which to sub-merge themselves. As these incidents often happen at night, it's un-derstandable that the hippo didn't see how steep the sides were. I have also heard of young elephant, and even buffalo, falling into swimming pools. In all these instances the victims were members of herds, thirsty for water during unusually dry times. When a lot of thirsty animals gath-er at a small waterhole, there is often much jostling for place and it is easy to imagine how an animal straining for water over the lip of the swimming pool could be nudged from behind, sending it crashing into the water with a wide-eyed splash and conveniently raising the water level for its companions.

I have yet to hear of lions, leopards, African Wild Dogs or any other large predators stumbling into a swimming pool.

But the hyaena was in our swimming pool.

I believe I solved the mystery a couple of days later.

I went to my museum, which was just beyond the last safari tent on the outskirts of the camp, for a brief inspection and to dust the cob-webs that would have been added to the décor. I had not been to the museum for some days and, when I arrived, was horrified to find a specimen missing.

The salad bowl lay on its side on the floor, my paper inscription torn and the vodka drained. I was unable to find even a single scale of my beautiful Puff Adder.

Old, but still visible in the sand outside were hyaena tracks.

That's when it all became clear.

A hyaena – *the* hyaena – had found the museum during its evening's prowling. The pickled Puff Adder had smelt like a legitimate source of food. The bowl had been dragged across the table until it had crashed to the earthen floor below. The wet snake had been removed from the bowl and eaten, probably a new and exciting flavour, making an inter-esting change from just plain raw meat.

The problem is: Alcohol makes you thirsty. Imagine the drunk hy-aena straining to get its head down below the lip of the swimming pool for a desperately needed drink. . .

Heavy Summer Eyes

Six weeks of game drives, morning and evening, can be tiring, especially in the middle of January when the lowveld is a constant, sweaty swelter. The animals seem content to hide for days in the lush summer bush to wait out the heat. There are a number of stories of rangers being overcome with the fatigue from hours of trying to entertain guests who are not seeing what they want to see. Some become experts at hiding the fact that they are taking forty winks while their guests watch animals. A ranger might place his elbow on the seat frame behind him and then subtly rest his face against his hand, so obscuring his eyes. He can then watch his lids while his guests watch the animals.

There are two instances when such a ploy may result in embarrassment. Firstly, the ranger might wake with a start, knowing that he has been asked a question but having no idea what it was. Normally he will take a gamble with some random piece of biology and steer his answer in the right direction according to the look on the questioner's face. Secondly, his elbow might slip resulting in a loud 'ding' as his skull hits the seat frame behind him.

One particularly hot and bothersome afternoon a ranger and his tracker were searching for rhino. There was nothing to be seen except the odd desert-adapted Crowned Lapwing. The ranger was exhausted from trying to amuse his guests who, every time he turned around, looked at him with scorched disgust. Gradually his eyelids began to droop.

Out of the blue the vehicle lurched off the road into a Flaky Thorn thicket. The tracker leapt across the bonnet in an effort to shield his face from the thorns. The hitherto silent guests yelled in surprise as the ranger, woken by crashing noises, managed to right the car.

'Ah,' said he, suddenly wide awake and looking at the road next to him, 'fresh rhino tracks, what a spot of luck!'

'Oh,' said the guests suspiciously, as the Land Rover sped off before the tracker could examine the road.

James Hendry

In search of the Ornithological Grail

(The Okavango Delta panhandle, Botswana)

by CHRIS ROCHE

I began enjoying bird-watching by the age of five and used to join my father on weekend trips to the nearest wetlands where I quickly racked up a life list with a bias towards waterfowl. I had been lucky enough to see a Grass Owl and regularly saw Marsh and Barn Owls. A Spotted Eagle-Owl followed in a suburban garden, while the Verreaux's and African Wood-Owls, the Southern White-faced Scops-Owl and the Pearl-spotted and Barred Owlets came after visits to wilder climes. The cryptic African Scops-Owl and habitat specific Cape Eagle-Owl were always going to be difficult, but the Pel's Fishing-Owl was really what I was after. From Peter Steyn's *Birds of Prey of Southern Africa* I knew its southern African stronghold to be the Okavango and longed for a chance to visit the legendary swamps.

Many years later my chance came. I wasn't the primary guide on this occasion, but relished the opportunity to join a group specifically interested in Okavango birding and, of course, the elusive Sitatunga – an antelope specifically adapted to life in wetland areas. We started in the panhandle at a lodge known for its birding opportunities and were not disappointed, with lifers for all of us Delta debutantes coming thick and fast. Western Banded Snake-Eagle, Long-toed Lapwing, African Skimmer, Coppery-tailed Coucal, Hartlaub's Babbler, Swamp Boubou and Brown Firefinch were all new and exciting birds for us and we gloried in spectacular views of other great birds set against a backdrop of lush riverine woodland, river channel and vast tracts of papyrus. The first and last of these habitats harboured the two most sought after species however, and despite exhaustive searches of all the known local roosts and even an old nest site of the Pel's we had come up agonisingly short on that count. A number of early morning and late afternoon trips along the river hoping to surprise a Sitatunga proved more fruitful however, and we had good views of a single adult male making his way across some papyrus and then splashing into a quiet backwater where we lost sight of him.

One down and one to go was the thought that lingered in the backs of all our minds on the last afternoon. We opted not to explore the water on this occasion and rather to comb the riverine woodland that lined the western bank of the Okavango on foot. Roost and nest sites of the Pel's are known to be found in thickly foliaged trees in just these sorts of conditions, and the area around the camp and extending south along the river was generously endowed with extensive stands of Jackal-berry, Sycamore Fig and African Mangosteen. It was through these trees that we searched, the local guide and camp manager Jonathan leading the way out of the camp, whereupon we all spread out and wandered through the riverine strip, necks craned backward and eyes upward as we peered into the dark canopy. A commotion of agitated babblers, bulbuls and a Tree Squirrel instantly raised our hopes, only for us to have them dashed as we found a boomslang instead of an owl in the branches of a mangosteen.

Two hours later we had still not turned up a Pel's. Jonathan then led us in single file along a path down by the river. The camp was situated at the tip of a bulbous peninsula and aside from a few hundred metres directly on the river, the edges of the area immediately around the camp bordered on papyrus. Adjacent to this papyrus was lower-lying riverine woodland with water from the river penetrating into small hollows. Beneath the figs and Jackal-berry trees it was dark, with filtered sunlight dappling the forest floor and its multi-coloured leaf litter: perfect for Pel's and the kind of place you could imagine a leopard sauntering through in the middle of the day. Leopards were not on our mind though as we followed Jonathan along the path, focusing doggedly on our objective. Jonathan – now under pressure to produce what a couple of days ago he had been pretty confident of providing –

was at the head of our single file, with me just behind him. Without exception we were all staring into the canopy, using only the briefest of downward glances to make sure we weren't going to trip on any obstacles.

Suddenly Jonathan leapt back almost onto me with a sharp yelp. I immediately looked down at what he stared in shock at, and saw only a log. That was all he had seen as well, until he stepped on it and found it instead to be a large female Southern African Python lying very still across the path. She still had not moved by the time I picked out her form in the shadows, but as we crowded together on the path to have a look at her she slowly began to move down towards a water-filled hollow on our right. It was a primeval scene – the enormous, apparently unconcerned snake, leisurely moving away from the cause of disturbance and slowly sliding into the protection of the dark water. As she had moved off, we noticed for the first time a tangle of other pythons around the area where her tail had been. We estimated her to be almost five metres in length, but these pythons were much smaller and all measured between two and three metres. Aside from two or three on the outer fringes, all six or seven pythons were intertwined or at least touching each other. A bizarre sight, and one made all the more spectacular by the unexpectedness of the experience.

As we drank in the scene before us, the tangle of smaller pythons gradually – almost in slow motion it seemed – disentangled and melted away in different directions below the understorey of a Large Feverberry tree. The late afternoon quiet, in a dark and gloomy woodland, exacerbated the surreal nature of the experience and we hardly spoke as we moved on, furtively glancing backward, in the direction of the now invisible female. By the time we had covered the remaining few hundred metres to the camp we remembered that we were supposed to have been looking upward for the Pel's. Despite missing out on the rare owl we were exhilarated by the intimacy of our experience, which proved not to be covered in any of the reptile field guides at the camp.

Theories abounded. That the smaller pythons must have been the offspring of the larger female was a strong contender. Maternal care could surely not last so long in reptiles, was the immediate rejoinder. We certainly were intrigued though and only on consultation with a reptile park when passing through Johannesburg did we discover that the larger python must indeed have been a receptive female and that her condition had attracted all the local males with the intention of mating with her.

Careful with my Corvette, *s'il vous plaît*

Mademoiselle Eloise got on famously with her ranger, Michelle. She invited her to her home in France, promising to look after her and facilitate her explorations of the countryside.

When the elephant charged the Land Rover, Michelle had to take prompt action. She turned off-road, crashing through bushes and small trees and bouncing over the uneven terrain as fast as she could, in an effort to escape the enraged beast. Only when, finally, the elephant relented, could she turn around to see how her guests were. She feared that they would have been badly rattled by the experience.

Mademoiselle Eloise shrugged off the concern on Michelle's face, but added a stern proviso to her offer: 'If you do come to Paris, you're not driving my car!'

David Hood

Bushpilots!

(In and above the Okavango Delta)

by DAVID HOOD

I am sitting at the Duck Inn*, a little restaurant overlooking Maun Airport. In the Botswana heat, it is a welcome place to cool off and fill up. Looking through the mesh fencing at the tiny airport building it is difficult to believe that this is the airport that hosts more take-offs and landings than any other in the Southern Hemisphere . . . Sitting on the wooden benches of the 'Inn', you can watch an almost constant stream of light aircraft coming and going.

Bushpilots!

Don't be fooled, you may think you have met a normal, perhaps even civilized bushpilot. You'll shake hands on the smouldering tarmac and he'll smile charmingly at you. While you are studying the rivets that hold the thin metal sheets of the wing together, he'll allay your fears with his complete ease. He'll help you into the plane, reminding you not to bump your head on the overhead wing. He'll run through the safety brief making it sound ridiculously simple. He may or may not mention the paper packets behind the seat, but you'll find them anyway. You'll taxi down to the end of the runway while he talks into his headset above the roar of the propeller. He'll press a few buttons, pull a lever and you'll charge off into the sky.

---

* You can still go to the Duck Inn today, only now it's called the Bull and Bush. You can sit in the shade of a thatched roof and drink a 'cooly' while watching these shiny contraptions with their mad pilots come and go. You may be a little surprised to hear the odd person refer to the restaurant as the Bullet and Bush: Just hours after the Bull and Bush's debut calzone was served, an irate fellow with a hunting rifle blew away a relative he disagreed with, hence the name. The fact that he did it just outside the restaurant had nothing to do with the food.

During the flight, he'll point out interesting features, maybe tip the plane a little to give you a view of a herd of elephant down below. At the other end, he'll land neatly on the dirt strip and you'll bounce and rattle to a halt ahead of a billowing cloud of dust. He'll open the door for you, smile and ask if you enjoyed the flight. He'll hand you over to your ranger, whose neatly polished four-wheel drive is waiting patiently on the edge of the strip.

Then without further ado, he'll wave goodbye, hop back into his little craft and pull the door closed. He'll put on his headphones, give you the thumbs up and fire up the engine. As his metal bird rises above the trees, the sound of its engine will be replaced by the zing of cicadas and you'll be left wondering what all the fuss is about.

Indeed, what *is* all the fuss about? The bushpilot is a professional in every sense of the word. If you are a paying guest in his aeroplane, he will deliver a neat, impeccable service.

But wait . . . what if you are not a paying guest in his aircraft, what if you are just someone who works at a camp, getting a lift with him? He'll consider you a compatriot and if he has time on his hands, he'll turn to you – as he has done to me – and shout over the drone of the engine, 'Should we have a bit of fun?'

He'll grin, trying hopelessly to hide the mischievous curl at the corner of his mouth and you, not knowing any better, will nod your head and shout back, 'Why not?'

He'll adjust his headphones slightly, turn and look at the other passengers in the seats behind to make sure that they are all strapped in. He'll give them a thumbs up and without further ado, ram the unsuspecting aircraft into a death-defying dive. You'll be clutching the sides of your seat, watching as little green dots rapidly become respectable trees. You'll see warthog and impala materialise on the hard ground below and dash away in panic. Your wide-eyed gaze will be transfixed ahead, watching brown spots become towering termite mounds, so you won't see the pilot glance in your direction and grin smugly to himself before pulling back on the controls and taking a gap between two tree islands.

Next he might take you at giraffe-height out towards the floodplains. Without warning the ground will disappear from beneath you, to be replaced by a shimmering lagoon that glints with the sun's reflection.

A pod of hippo will splash and lurch in a frenzy of bulky panic, sending waves across the calm surface. But, the pilot, seeing that you are starting to relax and enjoy the ride, takes it down a level. Now you are flying just above the reedbeds of endless swampland and a rush of vertigo makes your head spin. If you look to the side, you might see a herd of Red Lechwe bounding and splashing through the shallow water. The droplets of spray glisten in the sun and you are almost at eye level with the wet antelope.

The pilot sees that you are no longer clutching your seat and decides to remedy that. He pulls back sharply on the controls. Your internal organs rearrange themselves. The drone of the engine changes pitch as the little aeroplane fights its way upward. You glance out of the side window to see where the ground has gone. As you strain to look backwards and catch sight of it, it disappears and you are blinded by the sun. *Is everything all right?* You look quickly to the pilot but see only rapidly approaching ground twisting in the window behind him. Another twist and you are headed straight for the ground again.

You know this one, you've done it before. As you glare sideways at the sadistic pilot, he smiles back. You just glare and realize you don't feel right. The pilot now has you where he wants you and he levels out in another ground-scraping dash. Only this time, the reeds end in an impenetrable wall of trees. It's obvious – he's going to wait until the last minute before he pulls up.

You sit back and brace yourself for a nauseating rise. But he just keeps going and you start to worry. Before you know it, all you can see above the mass of dials in front of you, are trees. You can see them really well, lots of them, towering above the charging plane. *Is he mad, what's he doing?* You glance at him and he knows he's got you. With a gleeful grin he pulls back and twists the controls. The aircraft contorts impossibly and you are trying desperately to keep breakfast down as the canopy drops away beneath you.

Finally, you can see the airstrip ahead and you touch down on solid ground. The minute the spinning rotor comes to a stop, you have the door open and stumble out onto the hard dirt of the airstrip.

You have no desire to climb back into the plane; you have no reason to trust a bushpilot ever again . . . but you have to admit, it was a little bit fun!

Because the error margins are so small in flying as compared to, for instance, riding a bicycle, pilots have to adhere to certain strict disciplines. Logbooks must be completed, services done regularly, pre-flight checks carried out religiously. Then there are the two commandments: no drinking eight hours before flying and no smoking within eight metres of the aircraft. These rules are strictly adhered to, (though some pilots insist the first commandment is 'no drinking within eight metres of the aircraft').

Late at night, once the precious machines have been put to bed, there is no need for regimental efficiency and there are no rules! The aircraft have been lovingly placed in their spot on the tarmac, wings secured with anchor ropes in case of wind in the night and it is time to celebrate surviving another day. This is when Maun's feral donkeys are ambushed in the dark and ridden, braying and bucking. Women, blindfolded, will be challenged to identify which pilot is which, based entirely on the feel of his bare bottom. Alcohol will be consumed and dreams of flying jumbo jets will be discussed. Eventually, the tired and unstable captains of their ships will stumble homewards and an uncertain peace will settle over the little town.

Bushpilots lead charmed lives – *most* of the time. Flying a metal bird is a fine operation, and a small error can become a fatal one.

At our little camp in the Okavango, we were dependent on air transport. The drive to town was arduous and when the floodwaters were high, it was simply not an option. Guests and fresh food always flew in to camp. Staff too, usually flew in and out as did news of the outside world. Real news was often sprinkled with a peppering of gossip that travelled on the lips of the pilots, who knew it all.

From the camp, you could just make out the sound of aircraft taking off and landing if the wind was right. If the pilot knew there were no guests at the lodge, he might fly low past camp and waggle his wings in greeting. In the distance too, we would sometimes see little Cessnas or bigger Caravans on their way to another concession.

Then, one pleasant sunny day, I was a little way from the camp with a few of the staff, building a causeway. We wanted a fordable crossing that would bridge a narrow section of floodplain before the floods came.

The annual floodwaters of the Okavango delta usually reach this concession in April or May. They travel from afar, originating in the mountains of Angola where it rains months before. Streams become rivers and rivers join forces to become the Kavango. The swollen Kavango carries its gift from the heavens across Namibia's narrow Caprivi Strip and into the panhandle of the delta. This precious water courses through the panhandle and is released to form a myriad of ever changing channels that is called the Okavango.

The water edges its way along dry channels and creeps among the dry grasses of ancient floodplains, bringing life to a multitude of living creatures and reviving countless plants before disappearing back into the earth. It spends its last droplets holding back the mighty dryness of the Kalahari and then recedes slowly.

But when this mosaic of channels and floodplains rose above the dry grass and dead reeds around our camp, it would cut us off from considerable areas of the concession. The causeway we were building would link two roads on either side of a long system of floodplains.

So there we were with shovels and picks, digging holes to put gum pole anchors in.

This crossing-to-be was close to the airstrip and while we were working, an aeroplane landed. It didn't stay for long and we could hear the distant hum of its engine getting ready for take-off. Next we heard it speeding along the strip, the sound changing subtly as it went. We heard it take off, the pitch of its engine changing again and becoming a little clearer. These were familiar sounds and we took little notice.

Then, as one, we stopped our work. The low drone of the aircraft had stopped in mid-verse. Instead of the comforting buzz of the engine, there was only a most chilling silence.

I felt prickles of dread race back and forth across my body. It seemed like a few seconds that we waited before the silence was punctuated by a thud. It was a dull thud in the distance but clearly audible. It was followed, brutally, by more silence. We listened for a second longer, irrationally hoping that we had misheard.

I looked around me at the wide eyes, all staring in the same direction. I looked at our two vehicles parked off at the edge of the floodplain and I imagined horrible scenarios.

'*Ari!*' (Let's go!) I turned and jogged towards the vehicles. As we went, I was trying to visualise where the plane would be, at the same time formulating a plan of action. I chose a couple of men to come with me. The rest were to go quickly back to the camp, which was only a few minutes' drive away, tell the manager what had happened and bring him back, along with all the first-aid equipment.

As I powered the vehicle through the thick sand of the track, imagining flames, wreckage and broken bodies, I radioed the camp. The manager's voice answered immediately.

'Darren, did you hear that?' I asked.

'Hear what?'

'It sounded like a plane went down somewhere east of the airstrip; we're on our way to have a look. Phillip is on his way to the camp with the other vehicle, he should be there in a couple of minutes.'

'Copy that, I'll come as soon as the vehicle gets here.

'Copy, thanks . . . don't forget the first-aid boxes and the spinal board . . .'

'Copy.'

The actual aircraft took us by surprise. It was closer than we anticipated.

'Darren, come in,' I called.

'Go ahead.'

'They are in the lagoon near the airstrip, could you bring a *mokoro*?'*

* dugout canoe

'Copy, we'll load one up.'

We looked at the aeroplane and despite everything, we chuckled. It was an eight-seater Cessna and it was right-way-up in water that lapped at its windowsills. The left wing was bent and half of it had been torn right off. The metal cover above the engine was buckled but the rest of the fuselage seemed to be in reasonable condition.

The pilot and four guests were huddled on the roof between the wings. We chuckled out of sheer relief to see everyone in one piece. They waved at us. We waved back and drove around to the closest access point. I parked the Landcruiser on a patch of short hippo-mown grass and we jumped out. The resident hippos grunted their objections from the far side of the lagoon. I smiled inwardly. They too had had a traumatic experience; in fact they usually spent the day about where the aircraft was now. I wondered briefly how close they had been when the plane hit the water.

I walked to the edge of the lagoon, scanning the reeds for crocodiles and shouted across the water. I was still concerned that there might be some internal or back injuries that were not obvious, perhaps even to the victims, who would be in shock after such an experience. 'We're okay!' came the reply.

'Someone is coming with a *mokoro*, wait there, he'll be here very soon!' I shouted.

I radioed Darren to let him know that there were no serious injuries. He had almost reached us.

The pilot, however, decided they could not wait and plunged into the chest-deep crocodile habitat. He helped the passengers in after him. Some of them even carried items of luggage above their heads. So much for the responsible pilot!

Oh well, I thought, there's nothing for it, and I waded out through the reeds to help them. My companions kept their feet firmly on dry land – they knew what lurked in those waters. That sort of reedbed is exactly where a skulking crocodile would lie up – good cover and a perfect view of the lagoon!

I met the sodden group in the water, still unimpressed by the pilot's

bravado, and took as much luggage as I could. I had already met the guests at the lodge and through a few subdued exchanges gathered that they were rattled but in reasonable spirits. One of the women had had an earring ripped out – it had caught on the seat back – and one of the men had a small gash on his forehead. The others seemed unscathed.

Darren arrived with two *mokoros* strapped to his vehicle. First-aid containers were unloaded and I bandaged the man's gash while Darren and the pilot retrieved the remainder of the luggage. I finished wrapping a triangular bandage around the injured man's head, turning his respectable pate into that of an unlikely buccaneer. He thanked me politely anyway.

The pilot explained to us that the engine – which was in fact almost brand new – had simply stopped shortly after take-off. He had aimed for the most open piece of ground he could see, which just happened to be on the far side of the lagoon. Taking a gap between towering Lala Palms, his craft had fallen short and just missed a few hippos.

Darren got on the radio to camp and organised another flight out. As it happened, a Cessna 206 was on its way with freight and the guests could go out on that one. They would be taken to Maun Hospital and X-rayed for back injuries before catching their next flight.

Perfect.

The last of the sodden luggage was collected and guests were helped onto the vehicle. Darren drove them to the airstrip, where they would wait while we packed up and went back to camp for towels and to raid the curio shop for dry T-shirts.

We arrived at the airstrip after the Cessna had touched down and handed out dry clothing. There was another aircraft waiting on the strip and other guests waiting to depart. Like it or not, they were getting the gory details shortly before getting into a plane themselves.

The second aircraft was an Islander, a much bigger twelve-seater with overhead wings, each bearing a single propeller. Islanders are ugly box-shaped planes but excellent for short take-offs.

We waited while the last items of luggage were loaded. We waited while people milled about around the planes. We waited and waited and I began to wonder what was wrong. Usually pilots are very efficient, luggage is loaded, passengers are briefed and strapped in and they are off. The crash victims had agreed that they were happy to fly again, so what could possibly be amiss?

There was more milling about and then, finally, shapes climbed into the Islander, doors were shut and its twin engines roared to life. With whirring rotors, it taxied onto the runway ahead of a cloud of dust. It turned and began its sprint along the hard dirt surface. We waved at the little windows as the great metal contraption parted ways with its faithful shadow. Not far behind, the Cessna followed suit, running further down the strip before taking to the air.

Dust settled and peace returned. Insects and birds called as if nothing had ever happened.

Back at the camp, Darren revealed the cause of the delay. The two aircraft belonged to different companies and therefore had different schedules. A whole lot of reorganising had had to take place because the wet crash victims had taken one look at their little Cessna, one look at the bigger Islander and resolutely made up their minds.

They were going in the big one – the one with two engines!

Safety in Colours

'Aposematic colouration' – the use of bright colouration by an animal species to warn potential predators of toxic tissues or secretions in that species, or simply to alert a hunter to its less than palatable taste – protects such species and allows them to forage unhindered.

Butterflies provide a classic example of this, and many of the toxic and unpalatable *Acraea* species, as well as the well-known African Monarch, display very bright, orange and red colouration. So successful is this phenomenon that it has spawned a myriad of mimics – the female of the Common Diadem for example rendering itself almost an exact replica of the monarch.

This is not the only way in which insects and other animals use bright colours to protect themselves from predators and other unwanted attention. Grasshoppers bring another method to mind. While some species, such as the Elegant Grasshopper, certainly do employ bright colours (yellow in this case) to warn predators, other (not necessarily unpalatable species) use bright wing colours that are displayed only in flight. These species, when under threat, wait until the last minute before breaking cover and opening their wings, thereby providing a bright colour for the predator to focus on. After a short, fast flight they close their wings and disappear into the grass, their drab bodies blending perfectly with the tangle of grass stems and forbs.

Instead of allowing the predator to form a good visual picture of their actual colouration and shape, these grasshoppers have forced the predator's mind to think of them as brightly coloured. The grasshoppers now sit tight and display only the disruptive pattern of muted colours on their thorax and wing casing.

A similar mechanism is found in some larger mammals. Greater Kudu, Common Reedbuck, Oribi or even Scrub Hares, for example, all flee from predators with the white underside of their tails prominently displayed. This is usually explained as a following mechanism allowing members of the herd to follow each other and maintain safety in numbers and it no doubt does serve something of this function. It might seem counterproductive however when there is a chasing predator to consider: Why provide this animal with something to focus on and follow?

Much like the grasshopper example, the attentions of a potential predator are now focused on the brightest object in front of them – reds or yellows in the case of grasshoppers, whose main predators are birds, which have colour vision, and white in the case of the mammals whose main predators are other mammals capable only of seeing in black and white. As soon as the fleeing kudu, or zigzagging hare has reached cover (dappled riverine shade in the former case and low, scrubby vegetation in the latter), the tail is folded down and the predator's target instantly disappears, the camouflage of the erstwhile prey now coming into effect and allowing it to blend into its surroundings.

Without this beacon to focus on, the predator needs to reacquire prey shape and colouration, wasting precious time, often enabling the quarry to escape unnoticed.

Chris Roche

Another Story

(Where Marulas Grow, Grey Giants Wander)

by DAVID HOOD

I woke up in the night. Something had disturbed my sleep, for I was wide awake, not groggy or disorientated. Outside the gauze windows of my substantial tent all was darkness – an unfamiliar darkness, as I had only recently taken up residence in my new quarters at my first official job in the bush.

I listened. Yes, there was a noise, it was a soft muffled sound repeated in a rhythmical but slightly irregular sort of way. I recognised the sound – it was grass being pulled and broken – but did not know what was making it. Could it be an elephant, I wondered. No, an elephant would pull up a swath of grass and then chew on it, an elephant would not munch with the regularity of what I was hearing.

It munched closer and I began to worry. The munching was accompanied by an occasional low snuffle. Could it be an antelope or zebra? It sounded, somehow, much bigger. No, it wasn't an antelope, no antelope would eat that much grass that quickly. Whatever it was, it seemed to be munching determinedly towards my tent.

I felt the first twinges of fear. I was in a *tent* – a big animal could easily flatten it or tear a hole in it with a horn or tusk. I thought about turning on my bedside light, but then I thought: What would that do? I still wouldn't be able to see through the mesh of the windows, and the animal, whatever it was, might get a fright and attack. I usually kept a big knife at my bedside but I had started to relax that discipline. Where was it now? Was it under my bed or had I left it on the other side of the tent?

The munching was close now. I began to plan my escape in the event of an attack. I would have to roll off my bed quickly because it was up against the side the muncher was approaching. Then I'd make a brief dash for the entrance. I'd have to find the zip in the dark and get it open fast. I hoped the creature wouldn't go around and block me off on that side. Once outside, I'd run for the closest solid structure, which was the little shower building twenty metres away. It was nothing more than a thatched structure with thin reed walls, but it felt somehow more sturdy than my tent.

The munching persisted, nearer and nearer. My whole body tensed, ready for action. I felt a panicked need to know what I was up against. What about a buffalo? Maybe it was a buffalo; they ate a lot of grass. But that didn't seem right; I hadn't seen any buffalo near the camp.

It must have been metres away now. Then I realised: It's a hippo! It must be a hippo – they graze at night and the water was not far away.

Knowing it was a hippo didn't help – the biggest killer of humans in Africa was only metres away and all that separated me from this monster was a sheet of canvas. This was not good! I got ready to whip the duvet off and tried to keep calm. I would need to have my wits about me when the canvas began to contort under the angry hippo's whim. I must find the entrance quickly, even if it was moving.

It was loud now, and getting louder, and then: 'Duh!' My whole tent shuddered. I lay frozen, waiting for the hippo's next move.

Beyond the canvas there was only silence. The first silence stretched out into a string of terrible smaller silences. I tried not to breathe. I knew what had happened: the hippo had walked into one of the poles that supported the tent. They were about half a metre from the side and it must have walked into the one closest to my pillow. Perhaps if the canvas wall had not been there, I could have rolled over and touched the bristles on its big muzzle.

I did not know if the hippo would be upset about the tent being in its way – or about the pole. The heavy silence told me nothing, except that the hippo was not scared and that it was deciding what to do next. I waited, feeling the terrible unknown press down on my chest. I dared not flinch lest a bedspring creak or a sheet rustle.

Then, just as suddenly as it had come, the silence disappeared. It was replaced by a snuffle and a 'munch' and, I thought, the scuff of a big hoof. The munching continued, rhythmically, repetitively and my life was spared. I felt relief sparkle through my limbs and balloon in my chest. None of my emergency plans had been called into action, nor would I need a new tent. For the first time, I enjoyed the fading sound of munching.

'Munch . . . Munch . . . Munch.'

I had just had a tangle of misconceptions banished forever. I had learnt a great lesson.

My second tutor gave me little time to digest the lessons of my first. He strode into the camp in all his majesty and he demanded my attention. Of course he did – he was an elephant!

It was during February and March of that year that the marula trees fruited. I made a note of that because it was the first time I had seen marulas fruiting and I wanted to compare things from year to year.

The elephant that came into our camp was braver than the rest. He made no excuses for coming, he never apologised and he ate all the marulas.

There were only a few female marula trees in our camp – the male trees produce pollen only and are therefore of little interest to an elephant. Of those few trees, one was particularly big. Its grand boughs branched high above the little thatched shower building and its copious fruit fell with an audible thud, right onto my tent roof!

Marula fruit ripen on the ground where animals – particularly elephant – can get to them easily, eat them and take their hard seeds elsewhere. The hard green fruit rolled off my tent roof and littered the area around my flimsy home where they quickly ripened to a glowing yellow, irresistible to any fruit eater.

At first the elephant came in the dark when I was already in bed. I know because I saw him. I always left the heavy canvas flaps of my tent entrance open because of the heat. The gauze flaps kept the insects out while letting the breeze in. When the light was off inside the tent I could see through the gauze; I could see things like elephants.

Mostly I could just hear the elephant when he sucked air through his trunk to gather marulas, but sometimes he would come and stand right in front of my tent. From the comfort of my bed I could see little through the gauze flaps except elephant. He made everything dark except for the space beneath his belly and between his legs, through which I could see moonlight shining on leaves and branches.

I felt awed to have such a magnificent creature in such close proximity, but, initially at least, I wished he wouldn't come quite so close. Soon however, I realised that, like the hippo, he was not out to get me, and I began to enjoy his close company, sometimes even falling asleep to the sound of him feeding.

As the marula trees unburdened themselves of ever increasing amounts of fruit, the elephant began to venture into the camp during the day too. He moved about in the leisurely manner of all elephants, but he worked diligently beneath the marulas, collecting as much fruit as he could and shovelling it into his cavernous mouth.

His presence, although always welcome, could also be something

of an obstacle. My bathroom, like my shower, was in a small thatched building. It was between this building and my tent that most of the marulas fell and, consequently, the elephant spent a significant amount of time here. Sometimes the bathroom, unlike the shower, could simply not wait, elephant or no elephant!

At first I gave him as wide a berth as I could, creeping through the bushes to the side of the pathway, ready to make a dash for it if I had to. I realised quickly that I was not deceiving him – he knew exactly where I was. Sometimes he would turn and look at me, sometimes he would breathe out with a whoosh when I came past. He was communicating in a language I did not understand, but I sensed that he did not want to be a threat to me. By gradual degrees of experimentation I discovered that I could walk past him just a few metres away. If he reacted at all to my presence, it was usually to take a step or two away.

I always tried to walk past bravely so that the elephant could see I was not afraid but inside I sensed that I was at his mercy. It is a terrifying thing to be at the mercy of an elephant!

In time – and not all that much of it – I began to see that the elephant did not treat everybody in the same way that he treated me. Many of the staff were so nervous when he was around that they would run if he so much as took a casual step in their direction. They seemed to annoy him and sometimes he would shake his head and flap his big ears at them. This instantly scared the living daylights out of them and made them squeal and scatter.

His irritable side was a considerable worry where guests were concerned. Usually we would make sure that guests were inside the lodge or bar building when he was around. Sometimes guests would actually need to be told that this was a *real* African Elephant. It seems incomprehensible that they could not *see* that, but perhaps they came from environments so modified and sterilised that they had forgotten any species, other than their own, could be dangerous.

I remember the day that a guest decided he didn't need to stay behind a solid structure. It was breakfast time. From behind the reed walls of the kitchen, the sound of sizzling sausages and bacon could be heard.

When the elephant came, breakfast was forgotten. We ushered all the guests either behind the bar counter or up the stairs into the lodge building. From our safe vantage points we watched the elephant's stately progress across the lawn. He stopped here and there to investigate something, or to look at all the people – far more people than he was normally used to. He ambled between the little thatched bar and the main lodge amidst a flurry of camera shutters. His steady progress took him behind the bar and out of sight of those in it.

To one middle-aged, grey-haired German photographer, this did not appear to be a problem. He came out of hiding and followed the mighty beast behind a hungry camera lens. Someone, probably his wife, shouted to him in German and he replied in words we did not understand, but the meaning of which was blatant. We watched in wonder as he crept closer and closer to the elephant, which was still moving slowly away. Perhaps he did not think that the elephant knew he was there, perhaps he assumed that it was a harmless gentle giant.

When he got to a distance of just less than twenty metres away, the elephant spun his towering grey bulk in a way that we would never have assumed possible and began walking quickly towards the photographer. The photographer was transformed into a sprinter and with camera in hand he disappeared from view. Seconds later we heard a chalet door slamming loudly and then silence.

The elephant left. There was nothing for it but to continue our breakfast and so we sat down, no-one commenting on the empty place. It was not until most of the guests were sipping their coffee, nearly half an hour later, that the German photographer crept back into the lodge on shaky knees and sat down for some sustenance.

It was clear to me that the elephant was not simply a benevolent marula-eating giant, he was also a very big, very strong African Elephant, well capable of aggression if his boundaries were violated. And yet, I was learning, his boundaries were flexible. I had walked past him at a far lesser distance than that which he had considered too close for the German photographer. Of course, I had simply been in urgent need of the bathroom, I had not been sneaking up on him and that, I suspected, was part of the reason he treated us differently. Animals, I began to perceive, have extremely limited vocal communicative abilities compared to us and consequently rely heavily on body language. I now believe that they react to nuances of human posture and movement that we ourselves may be oblivious to.

And there is more. This elephant occasionally chose to ignore, with me, the distances that I would have considered respectable between man and animal.

I remember, early one morning, having just finished my shower, I was preparing to brush my teeth when I heard a noise. It was coming from behind the reed wall of my bathroom. I froze and listened because it was close and I wanted to see what it was without frightening it away. I tried to focus beyond the gaps in the reeds to identify the culprit.

It is wonderful how little sound a five-ton elephant can make when he is a mere metre away. Through the gaps in the reed wall above the basin, I began to make out the shape of a tusk. The tusk was swaying gently and after a short while it moved forward and away from the wall. I watched for a bit and then decided to go ahead and brush my teeth. I was surprised that the elephant continued whatever it was that he was doing heedless of the commotion behind the reeds. He knew exactly where I was; even if I had not brushed my teeth, he had already heard me showering.

So there was a reed barrier between us – perhaps that was why he had felt comfortable in such close proximity to a human. It turned out that this was simply not the case.

Outside the back entrance to the kitchen was another marula tree. Here the marulas fell on a bare patch of ground that was a thoroughfare between the kitchen, the workshop and where most of the staff lived. On such thoroughfares the marulas were neatly raked into little piles along with any sticks and leaves that littered the area.

Some such piles were scattered about the area directly behind the kitchen entranceway and before they could be scooped into the wheelbarrow and carted away, the elephant found them. His appearance was preceded by ripples of mild panic. I watched him come and grabbed a few marulas from one of the piles. Pieces of juicy fruit in hand, I retreated to the kitchen entranceway, which was nothing more than a roofless break in a reed wall. There I waited feeling partially, but not entirely, safe.

The elephant slowed as he reached the cleared area, but he ignored the marulas. Stepping dexterously between them, he moved cautiously toward me. The biggest pile of marulas lay at my feet, just outside the kitchen and I wondered if perhaps he was coming to that pile. Perhaps he was but I don't believe it – he could have gathered far more from the other piles and by picking up individual fruit lying scattered in the surrounding bush without coming near me and the slightly larger pile at my feet.

He approached with little steps and movements of his trunk. It took all my self-control to stay where I was, pretending to be calm while my mind was furiously trying to interpret the elephant's intentions. He came close enough to take marulas from the pile near my feet, but he didn't – he watched me. He was close now, really close, and I was thinking, *what am I doing?* He could, if he'd wanted to, have lashed out and struck me with his trunk, or broken through the reed walls on either side of me and caught me in the open kitchen.

Watching him carefully, I tossed the marulas in my hand onto the pile on the ground nearby. He, like a reticent child who had just been given permission, stretched out his trunk and grasped some of the yellow fruit. As he began to feed, he moved a little closer and I watched as the prehensile tip of his trunk gathered the fruit unerringly and he curled the mighty appendage upward, emptying its load into his mouth.

His tusk at this moment in time was little more than half a metre from my head – the tip at my eye level. I studied the darkened cracks and wondered if I could react quickly enough if he decided to try and hook me. I was overwhelmed by his nearness but on some level believed that he would not hurt me.

After studying his tusk for a while, I ventured a look at his eye. I was afraid that staring directly into his eye would be confrontational, but I desperately wanted to know what was there. Turning my head excruciatingly slowly, I looked up at the dark, moist orb. Incredibly long black lashes curled down and then out from his upper eyelid. From behind this sparse curtain of wiry hairs, he was looking at me. He looked unblinkingly at me and I looked back, unblinkingly, at him.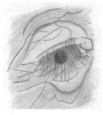

I could not see what was behind that dark eye but I did sense that there *was* something there. Something thoughtful, something sentient.

I know of no other person in that camp who shared with me such experiences and although I knew this was in part due to their own irrational fear, it made me think.

Slowly I began to form an understanding of what my silent tutor was teaching me. Sadly, I cannot confirm my experiences by any reference to a scientific work that statistically proves my perceptions. The best I can find in any of the modern, fanatically anti-anthropomorphic works of science are vague allusions that there may be more to animal cognisance than current research methods can fathom.

Perhaps part of the reason that human-animal relationships are not often explored in science is that those in a position to publish works of this nature generally belong to the large segment of society that has become isolated from nature. Even if this obstacle can be surmounted, in the political world of paper-publishing researchers, it is never a good career move to dabble in controversial ideas that cannot have numbers firmly attached to them as supporting evidence.

My understanding of the elephant's behaviour in relation to me, the human that lived under one of his favourite marula trees, does not need a lot of numbers – it is simple and although I cannot explain it the way an elephant can, I can at least endeavour to explain it in my own way.

I think it is all about behaviour – as I have mentioned – and it's all about territory. Of course, people behave differently on their own turf, just as animals behave differently within a territory they have taken possession of. The elephant is not a territorial animal. It does nevertheless have a home range beyond which it seldom ventures and there is a definite spatial organisation within an elephant herd. Without being territorial in the strict scent-marking and aggressively-defending sense of the word, I think elephant understand the concept.

And that is it! That is what I understood from the old bull's manner. The big marula tree was firmly in my territory – my scent (or perhaps my smell!) was strong in the area. I was intimately connected to that area and the elephant respected that by a lowering of his relative dominance – a between-species dominance. He tolerated me at a closer distance, and we related better, because he was not trying to assert his dominance or 'be the boss'. In fact, sometimes it was he that would back away from me.

On a slightly larger scale, a safari camp, albeit in the remotest corner of nowhere, has a sense of human ownership about it. Elephant are frequently less assertive in a camp than they are away from it. It is usually a relatively simple task to chase a naughty elephant out of a camp, and much easier than facing up to an elephant on unfamiliar ground. Of course, we, the chasers, feel more confident knowing the lie of the camp well and where to run to if the elephant behaves aggressively, but that confidence adds an element to our behaviour – part of the territorial advantage – that the elephant recognises and responds to.

These interlinked aspects of territory and behaviour are the concepts that help me to understand our relationship with elephant. Many of the same principles apply to our relationship with other species, but I am acutely aware that the elephant has more to teach me.

For now, I believe that my double territorial advantage, together with the elephant's love of marulas, brought us to a place of mutual respect. We were interested in each other's peculiarities and we co-existed happily because we both helped to balance the ever-compromising scale of respect. Except once.

Not altogether surprisingly, it was I, the human, who stepped over the line: Botswana was full of legends at the time I began working there. The legends were of brave men who tempted fate by catching enormous pythons and swimming with crocodiles. They crawled up to dozing lions and survived impossible encounters. And then there were those who stole the tail hairs from elephants!

Although I must confess that I am ashamed of it now, at the time I had no guide but these legends. I decided that in order to pursue a life in the bush I must be able to compete with these legends. I must take action. I must prove to myself that I can stand up to wild beasts the same way. Indeed, I must steal the tail hairs from an elephant!

This was decided a while before I had had most of my elephant encounters, long before I had formulated any discernable thoughts on territoriality, and so I was afraid. When I plotted to steal the thick cords of the elephant's tail, my palms and feet sweated because I knew I would be challenging a beast that could smash me to smithereens on a whim. Yet I felt compelled. If nothing else, I now needed to conquer the fear that I had created.

Then, before I had properly firmed my resolution, the elephant presented me with an opportunity. He came in the night to eat marulas. I would rather he had come in the day when I could see where to run, but he was there and I did not yet know he would come often. I was in two minds about his being in the camp: It was some comfort that I knew my way around and where the best places to run would be, but at the same time I envisaged an enraged elephant trampling chalets, tents, staff and guests as he gave vent to his anger at losing his tail hairs.

I was determined to follow it through and so I devised what I thought would be a cunning plan. In my tent was a pair of dissecting scissors that I had used the previous year for Zoology practicals. They had a cutting edge about as big as nail scissors and long handles. I thought that if I could cut his tail hairs instead of yanking them out, he would not notice and therefore not rampage through the camp killing innocent people. I would also not need to upset an animal I already felt affection for, but I would have snuck up as close as you can to a wild elephant and have the trophy to prove it.

Without further ado, I fetched my long-handled nail scissors and got into position. I watched the elephant from a safe distance. He was collecting marulas and I knew I must hurry because soon he would finish the fruit under that tree and move on to the next one.

It was late at night but a faint glow from the lodge beyond the trees and the moon above provided me with enough light. He was standing on the edge of a clearing facing away from the open space. That was not ideal because it meant there were no obstacles directly behind him to hide behind, but a short sprint would get me into the trees or to one of the thatched bathroom buildings. I felt a sense of urgency creeping up on me and began my approach.

Leaving the last cover, I circled around on the edge of the clearing to get directly behind the great pachyderm. At least the darkness afforded me some cover and the clearing meant there was less chance I would accidentally step on a twig or dry leaves.

He was moving slowly, turning slightly as he went and I moved to stay out of his sight. I started to cross the clearing. The stars blinked in the sky above and the leaves hung silently from their branches all around. I padded barefoot across the sand. Closer and closer I came to his bulk. There could be no turning back. His smell filled my nostrils and the sucking of his trunk roared in my ears. And now I was right behind him, trying to make out the fan of coarse hairs in the dark. I lifted the scissors and, anticipating the hairs would be difficult to cut, jerked the blades closed.

The elephant's reaction was instant. He turned to investigate. I too turned as soon as I saw the side of his big head. The elephant had forced me to choose between fight and flight. I decided on the latter – like a bullet!

As I ran I looked over my shoulder at the elephant. I noticed that he was not rampaging behind me, in fact he had hardly moved, save to turn and watch me with one eye as I fled into the darkness.

I stopped and looked back at the moonlit giant. He had not let out a single infuriated trumpet. Nor had he shaken his head in anger, slapping his huge ears against his side amidst a cloud of ghostly dust. He had simply turned and, flapping his ears slightly, exhaled loudly.

I watched him from the safety of the shadows and tried to fathom his unexpected tolerance. Was it that he couldn't see where I had gone? Did he recognise by smell or sight that it was me, who lived under his favourite marula, who had tweaked his tail? Was that why he did not break into an elephantine rage? I hoped not because that would mean I had betrayed a trust.

Whatever the reason, I avoided the old bull for the next few days. I suspected that he would be none too impressed with me. As much as I believed this, I could see no discernable change in his behaviour towards me. Eventually I had to conclude that he really did not bear a grudge at all. That made me feel worse for stealing his tail hairs.

Yet, that night, after I had challenged the big elephant and survived, I lay in my bed and, with eyes wide open, I dreamed of morning. I dreamed of the moment I would walk out onto the sand of the clearing and collect my trophy.

All in a Day's Work

(A Game Drive Extraordinaire)

by MEGAN EMMETT

Leopard, definitely leopard! And lion . . . and elephants . . . and what are the other Big Five again?' This is the standard answer I get when questioning newly arrived guests on what they would like to see during their stay in the bush. Smiling, I always assure them that we will be doing our best to see exactly what they have requested. It is their holiday after all. I then break into a cold sweat, knowing that from that moment on I have 48 hours to find these large yet elusive beasts. A precocious child once hit me with, 'I *wanna* see a pangolin', to which I replied, 'So do I!'

The inescapable daily challenge of a ranger is the task of finding game. Anyone who has visited a game reserve or national park will have experienced driving for long hours and seeing little. That's game viewing for you. It requires patience. For those happy to enjoy the birds, the 30-odd smaller mammal species in the park, bush smells and sounds, 'uneventful' drives are still rewarding and so the sight of an elephant or lazing lion rates as an additional treat.

Yet private reserves in places such as South Africa's lowveld or Kwa-Zulu-Natal are perceived as places where game viewing is easy. It is not uncommon to come across folk under the illusion that leopards and other big game wait in clear view for safari vehicles to happen past. Some game lodges have even marketed themselves as such, 'Come to our lodge and see the Big Five – guaranteed!' This certainly sets up the expectation that wild animals can be supplied 'on tap'. For us, the rangers, who have an average of four four-hour game drives to provide all of the desired creatures, the task can be a little tricky.

Granted, rangers have an intimate knowledge of the terrain through hours of walking in the bush, exploring every contour and drainage line and studying the ecology. Daily field trips develop an understanding of territorial animals' (such as lions and leopards) movements – at least we know where to begin the search. But on a large, unfenced reserve it is simply not a case of snapping one's fingers to produce game! Here enters the element of stress in the apparently 'stress-free' life of a ranger – employing each learned skill to produce a sighting in the shortest possible amount of time. (Breakfast is getting cold!)

In our ongoing attempt to present a rounded bush experience incorporating both the big-and-hairies and the smaller creepy-crawlies, some days just prove to be weighted towards the 'wow-factor' without our slightest effort. It is these blissful times that unfortunately perpetuate the myth that high profile game really is 'on tap' in private reserves. One particular afternoon comes rushing to mind.

Buffalo and Other Heavies

Leaving the lodge at the usual time, around twenty past four, well watered with tea and chocolate cake, we headed south along the main road into the mixed woodland terrain of the main game viewing area.

'What are we looking for this afternoon, folks?' I casually called over my shoulder.

'Buffalo!' came the united response.

This was the last of the 'Five' that we still needed to find and I had already determined this as my mission for the afternoon. The idea was to bide time while I furiously made mental decisions as to where the best place to look might be. After only fifteen minutes of slow yet purposeful ambling, a miraculous radio call rewarded my ears with the news that another ranger ahead of me had found a herd of buffalo crossing out of the reserve into an adjacent area. There are often no fences separating neighbouring concessions and while the rangers respect borders, the animals needn't.

'See if you can spot them,' I challenged the six excited faces behind me. We were quite a way off and keeping the intrepid safari-ers occupied with searching meant that we'd have a better chance of seeing them before they disappeared 'next door'. I was more than a little annoyed that after such a stroke of luck, the buffalo were evading me by going into an area where I couldn't follow.

I headed steadily in their supposed direction reaching the location minutes after the initial radio call. 'They're somewhere in here . . .' I said, waving my hand towards the thick wall of vegetation blocking our view eastwards. It was just unbelievable that four hundred 600 kg creatures had disappeared. I was puzzled by the absence of tracks, sounds or animals. Buffalo herds are living, thriving super-organisms. The wet-grass smell of their dung (like that of cattle) permeates the air around a herd and hovers in the atmosphere of places they pass through for days. The sound of fire moving through grass is the nearest to the noise their hooves and masticating jaws make, grasping and chewing at long grass while they move. Gentle bellows keep the herd members in contact and moving in the same direction as a unit. Their defence lies in one great black wall of bulk and bad temper. The little ones and cows don't wander far outside of the heart of the herd and the security of the bulls' peripheral protection. A proverbial tide of black-buffalo-sea ebbs and flows across the bushveld. Maybe I hadn't driven far enough along.

'Keep your eyes peeled,' I suggested to keep everyone part of the adventure. 'They have to be here somewhere!'

Continuing along the road, the missing-in-action bovids suddenly appeared right in front of the Land Rover, crossing back into our reserve. 'There they are!' came an eager shout from the back seat. Not that I was likely to have missed them but the guests were caught up in the search and enjoying it.

Returning in exactly the opposite direction they had travelled some 10 minutes previously, a long black row filtered out of the bush, slowly at first and then gradually with more urgency. The animals began to run. The strangeness of the spectacle was the fact that the entire herd was moving in a rank, one behind the other as if the road posed some kind of barrier and only one animal could pass at a time. Where a gap in the line formed, the animals would accelerate to catch up. We must have watched this ant-like row for twenty minutes with no sign of the end of the train.

'They're just as dumb as cows!' someone ventured in between the 'Ooh's' and 'Aah's'.

Being part of the Bovid family, African Buffalo are somewhat like cows, I explained, spending long hours of the day just grazing through long wild-grass pastures. The movement of hundreds of hooves and the feeding activities of so many animals trample grassland like a giant lawnmower. These areas then flush new shoots and produce short grass, available to species like zebra and wildebeest that prefer the shorter stems.

By this stage a gap in the black rank had formed wide enough for the Land Rover to dart through. 'I'm pretty sure they're going to drink. With this kind of urgency, they must be thirsty and there's a dam straight through there.' I pointed in the direction the buffalo were moving. 'Let's go round and meet them there.' Half a dozen nods approved.

Travelling steadily toward the dam to pre-empt their arrival, I passed through some open clearings riddled with general game, an unusual treat in these otherwise densely wooded parts – large numbers of giraffe, zebra, wildebeest, impala and warthog. After pausing to admire the spectacle, we carried on towards the dam, passing several more giraffe along the way. At the dam there was no sign of the buffalo yet but four hippos wallowed lazily in the grey water and an elephant bull drank noisily, making for entertaining viewing while we awaited the herd. 'All in a day's work,' I chuckled to myself. Sometimes this was blissfully easy.

Minutes later the stampede of thirsty buffalo arrived and blackened the drying watering hole like a plague of flies. A herd of drinking buffalo is a spectacular sight and the grunts, slurps and bellows mixed with the splashing and wet-cow smell is a delightful sensory experience. Several more 'ooh's', 'aah's' and 'wow's' emanated from my troupe of

excited guests. These grew in intensity as a small herd of elephant un-expectedly arrived and drank their share of the rapidly shrinking water-hole, keeping separate from the frenzied bustle of the buffalo.

Eyes darted from elephants to buffalo to hippo and back. A curious giraffe even crept up from behind us, also apparently hoping for a sun-downer drink but seeing this watering hole was just a little crowded with 'heavies', it decided to try elsewhere and moved away as quietly as it had arrived.

It hardly seemed possible but at that point the radio crackled to life. 'Stations, I've located a female leopard on a fresh impala kill in the Ma-rula section on Caracal Road.'

My mind began to race. We'd had an incredible afternoon of game viewing and I was reluctant to detract from the spectacle unfolding all around us by rushing off to see an animal we had seen that morning. Then the radio crackled again.

'Stations, this leopard has been treed by two lionesses who are now attempting to steal the impala out of the tree.'

No ways!

Usually the elevation of marula tree branches provides adequate sanctuary from such pirate attempts but these lionesses, a feisty mother-daughter duo, were apparently adamant that dinner was going to come easy tonight. From the radio reports, I followed the scenario but was still reluctant to whiz over there just yet. The lions fed in the tree for a bit forcing the poor leopard into the flimsy branches higher up in the crown. By the time the impala was dislodged and had crashed to the ground where the lionesses began to feed more seriously, I decided it was time to get across there before we missed any more of the action.

We arrived at the scene some 35 minutes later and the female leopard was still perched precariously in the tree's uppermost boughs, unable to do anything but hang on and watch her dinner being consumed before her very eyes! By now it was dark and after sitting a good while with these top predator competitors battling the eternal war of survival and supremacy, we headed home.

To our utter astonishment, another leopard lounged nonchalantly in a tree not far from where the first had been. Recognising this juvenile as the female leopard's male cub, I turned to six gaping-mouthed faces: 'This is the female's cub. It doesn't look like he'll be getting dinner tonight. If we don't get back to the lodge soon, neither will we!'

The somewhat rapid journey lodge-wards was interrupted consistently with stops for genets and chameleons in unusual proliferation, possibly as a result of the onset of summer, signalled by recent thundershowers. Nearing the lodge, another call came and I simply could not believe my ears.

'Stations, I have located a breeding herd of buffalo on the airstrip'.

The airstrip was just a few minutes from the lodge and I fancied that finishing the drive with a second viewing of the animal we had chosen as our afternoon's target would be a wonderful end to this fantastic drive. I had no expectation of what really awaited. Six lionesses were attempting to herd the enormous black beasts into a pen like sheep. Despite a degree of co-ordination and co-operation, their sheepdog efforts were futile, the practice of amateurs. Once the element of surprise is lost, there is no longer much chance of a successful kill as the buffalo form their clustered defence. Eventually the young lionesses seemed to realise this and they lay down and simply watched the herd, hungry but somehow aware of the inert danger of the buffalo's defence. Gradually the buffalo relaxed, instinctively aware of their upper hand. They too lay down, returning the lions' contemptuous stares.

We all stared as well. Mesmerised by this bizarre stand-off, mesmerised by all that we had seen in just one afternoon. All around us, embers glowed orange from a bushfire that had raged through the winter-dried grass, the smoke of which had stained the sunset more scarlet than usual.

Whether the guests on that Land Rover, upon whom nature had clearly chosen to smile, fully realised the magnitude of their privilege I'm not sure. What is sure, is that some days, this is the easiest (not to mention best) job in the world!

The Ancient Truth
(Why We Like it Here)

by JAMES HENDRY

Why do people spend time in wild places? Why do people choose to come to Africa?

Some never feel the yen to experience Africa. For them it is a continent of war, famine, corrupt governments, drought, heat and savage animals. Indeed, some guests' friends think they are saying good-bye forever as they watch the 747 lift off for the long flight to Johannesburg or Nairobi. Yes, we have all of these horrible things, and the saying that 'Africa is not for sissies' is a pertinent one, but for those of us who live here, they are not the most obvious defining characteristics of the world's most ancient land mass.

Guests from all over the Globe

In my time as a guide I have met people of all nationalities and personality types. I am forced to draw the conclusion that the hotchpotch of characters making up *Homo sapiens* makes us by far the most varied species in the world. As a guide I have had the pleasure of meeting people from all over the globe: Germans, Americans, Britons, Spaniards, Francs, Turks, one set of Malaysians, some crazy Russians, Brazilians, Australians, Kiwis, Indians, Swiss, Mexicans and of course South Africans. Although one can never generalise, allow me to light-heartedly relate some of the 'national characteristics' as I have experienced them.

It is apparent that all Spaniards over the age of sixteen smoke at least three packets of the vilest and most evil-smelling cigarettes legally procurable. They are jovial and extremely friendly travellers with little to no knowledge of English. Rangers usually know only one word of Spanish and that is *cerveza* (beer) which they will use in all situations as it is the only means of communication.

'*Buenos dias,*' says the eager Spanish guest. drawing on his fifth cigarette of the day as he ambles down for coffee at five in the morning.

'Ah yes, um . . . *Cerveza!*' says the ranger toothily.

The lack of mutually intelligible language can lead to some rather misleading conclusions. One night driving back towards the lodge a scrub hare sprang onto the road in front of us.

'*Leopardo!*' screamed the excitable Spanish couple.

'No, no,' I said as slowly as possible, 'scrub hare, like rabbit.'

'*Si, si, Leopardo!*' came the uncontrollably excited response.

I tried in vain to convince them of their error. As a final resort I climbed from the driver's seat and hopped up and down on the road Bugs Bunny style. This elicited shrieks of laughter and then a swift Latin rebuke because the 'leopard' had taken one look at me and fled.

Rangers tend to have a somewhat larger German vocabulary, with at least two words – *Achtung* and *schnell* – generally recognised. These are slightly more useful than *cerveza* as there are situations where both are applicable in the bush. When one is crashing through dense thickets with six-inch long white thorns threatening to remove eyes, the ranger can yell, '*Achtung, Achtung!*' which sends guests diving for safety under the seats.

But *schnell* comes in less handy, as it is not usually necessary to tell the very punctual Germans to hurry up. Some are wont to hurry things along when the ranger is lingering too long at a small animal sighting. Once we stopped to watch a flock of eight hooded vultures hopping around atop a termite mound, nabbing alates as they emerged on their nuptial flights. I was eagerly pointing and gesticulating when a tap on my shoulder arrested my exegesis: 'Ze big five, zen ze birdies,' said the guest, pausing for effect. '*Schnell!*'

The Americans I have guided have generally been extremely friendly and gracious. We have all heard about horrible American tourists, but evidently these sorts do not come to game reserves in South Africa. (Perhaps they are on those twelve-countries-in-six-days European vacations that pause only for refreshments at McDonalds). Our American guests are normally well read and interested in all aspects of ecology rather than just the big animals. Yes, there are some interesting questions asked such as: 'If it is November in the US, what month is it here?' but these are few and far between.

One of the fondest guiding experiences I have had was with a group of six Americans who were quite enthralled by every little piece of natural history I cared to share with them. We saw lions, leopards, wild dogs and all manner of other big game but they really wanted to see a giraffe. For three days we searched. Finally, on their last morning, just as we had given up the hunt we happened upon three stately bulls drinking at a pan. Despite the shadeless heat, I have never witnessed people more appreciative and mesmerised.

It was Noel Coward who said that only *Mad dogs and Englishmen go out in the midday sun*. The British never fail to turn up for the eleven o'clock walk in spite of the Saharan temperatures that prevail in January. It is probably the indomitable spirit of the empire that inspires such reckless behaviour. An hour later they are boiled to a fine beetroot red, some even hallucinating with dilated pupils. Perhaps it is just that they are so relieved to be out of the rain and mud at home that they feel the need to absorb as much sun as possible while they are here.

South Africans have the dubious distinction of being both the easiest and the most difficult to please. They are either especially well informed or totally clueless. There is naught more embarrassing than a huge, loud, fellow countryman sitting on the back of the Land Rover telling the ranger where to find animals and regaling the other guests with gross untruths.

'Dud you know vat ve elephants gets drunk on maroelas?'

'Um, what are marulas?' enquires the suspicious British guest who looks like he fears revenge is about to be exacted for the Boer War.

'Ya, vat one over ver,' says our expert pointing at an Apple Leaf tree.

Other South Africans, because they have experienced all the big game before, are happy to identify birds and plants and often just want to absorb the atmosphere. As for most return guests, they have graduated to another level of appreciation of nature. They simply crave the rejuvenating effect that it has on them.

Why come to Africa?

People who can afford to visit private game reserves are normally highly successful in their careers. They live high-intensity, high-pressure lives full of noisy technology, insistent communications and impossible deadlines. They work in uninspiring, manufactured surroundings under energy-sapping neon light.

To them, 'Africa' is a place of legendary romance and adventure. Although the luxury lodges that many choose do not really offer the same sort of roughing it that the explorers of old experienced, the animals, adventure and romance are still very much a part of the package.

Many people come here to live the experiences they have seen on television or read of in old hunting journals. For some it is purely Africa's large mammals that hold their fascination. Unfortunately a lot of people have been told to come and look for the 'Big Five'. This is quite possibly the most horribly-used marketing tool in ecotourism. So many say they want to see the 'Big Five' but have no idea of the term's origins or even which animals it includes. It is in fact an old hunting term that describes the most dangerous animals to shoot. It excludes fascinating creatures such as giraffe, zebra, hippo, cheetah and wild dog to name but a few. If you have any safari experience at all you cannot fail to notice how much more impressive a regal giraffe is than a fat comatose lion who does nothing other than role over once an hour to show you bits of him that you would rather not see anyway. How much more exciting is the sight of wild dogs on the hunt than a beaten-up old buffalo bull doing his business in a pool of mud and then lying in it?

One of the most exciting episodes I have ever experienced did not include one of the fabled 'Big Five' as a player.

We were driving west one winter afternoon when a pack of wild dogs emerged on to the road in front. There were just of four of them but we knew that they occupied a den full of hungry pups in the vicinity and were thus probably on the hunt. I was determined to impress my guests as they had come to Africa with expectations of high drama. More particularly, I was quite keen to make an impression on a dishy young American girl. With any luck all I would have to do was follow the dogs and they would do all the impressing.

I explained that we should stay with the pack as they were probably going to hunt. All agreed, with which the four lithe hounds spotted a herd of impala and careened off the road at top speed. I dropped a gear, told everyone to hold on tight and swung the Land Rover after them. Elvis, our tracker, guided us this way and that as he caught brief glimpses of the pack between the trees. After a time of furious off-roading, we lost sight of them. I switched off and told everyone to remain silent while we listened for contact calls from the hunters or alarm calls from their quarry. The afternoon was eerily silent.

My guests daubed the odd thorn cut and carefully removed handfuls of winter leaves from their hair and clothing. A yelp rang out just north-west of us and we tore off again, guests giggling with excitement and gripping the seat frames as we tore through the brush. A turbulent minute later, the trees parted to reveal a clearing as another sound greeted our ears. Three hysterically cackling hyaenas hurtled out of the setting sun. We skidded to a dusty halt in time to see a young impala break cover towards the scavengers just as the dogs grabbed her. The hyaenas wasted no time and charged in. In seconds the hapless antelope was torn to pieces and the two groups of predators dispersed to devour their portions. Heavy breathing was the only sound coming from the seats behind me. There was simply nothing to say as we absorbed the savagery of the scene.

Some guests appreciate all the creatures they come across, big and small. They are as fascinated by a little bushveld gerbil poking his head from a leaf-covered burrow as much as they are enthralled by the sight of an elephant dozing in the shade. They are captivated by the sight of a tiny Chinspot Batis incubating its clutch in a virtually invisible spider web- and lichen-covered nest or a chameleon's eyes peering in all directions as it clings nervously to a thin twig. They want to know why there are so many starlings living in the Mopane woodland or why the star Betelgeuse is red. For these there is a world of unlimited discovery open to them on safari.

In addition to the wildlife, many travellers wish to learn a little of the country's traditions and customs. South Africa has an extremely rich and turbulent cultural history. Guests' interests might lie in traditional plant usage or they may have an interest in how rural South Africans live. A visit to the local communities on the borders of the game reserve is a valuable lesson in the challenges facing rural villagers. These sorts of community trips have inspired a number of holidaymakers to give generously to development projects. Classrooms and clinics have been built, sport coached, conservation lessons imparted, bursaries awarded, water systems installed and medicines distributed, all on the funds that guests have donated to rural development. Cultural curiosity is also indulged by visiting historical sights on reserves or by experiencing traditional dancing and singing by the Shangane lodge staff.

Sometimes, after dinner had been served in the lodge boma, a select group of staff would gather outside. Mechanics, waiters, rangers, trackers and chefs donned semi-traditional Shangane outfits. For the men, skins around the midriff, white cattle-hair knee-flares, cow-hide shields and some rather frightening knob-topped sticks. The woman dressed in colourful skirts and headscarves and tied traditional rattles around their ankles. The drummer would beat his great cattle-skin instrument with extreme rhythmic violence and the group would march dramatically into the boma, singing, clapping and blowing whistles or kudu-horn trumpets. The vehemence of the troupe's entrance was such that the more nervous guests grabbed their loved ones and looked anxiously for the exit. For most, however, the traditional *Muchongolo* was a rare treat.

The group danced around the tables, ululating and smashing the drum deafeningly. As the big drum faded, smaller ones joined in and it was the turn of the women. Gentle drumming, clapping and singing drew the best dancers to the front where they moved around the fire lifting and skipping on one leg at a time, the shake of their rattles thickening the air. The last woman to dance was always Figness, dressed in a homemade hessian skirt strung with hundreds of bottle tops. She was the only one allowed to perform alone and when she did, her face taut with concentration, the guests went silent as she flew around in a haze of flailing legs and bottle tops.

Once she had finished, the men moved to the front into a high-energy, synchronized line dance. Legs would lift alternately, in time with the drum, kicking up a cloud of dust that combined with the orange firelight to blanket the scene with a dim mysterious glow. Every so often Aaron from the workshop would lose control of himself, leaping to the front of the group, and flinging himself about wildly before bounding from the floor and returning to his place. If he felt particularly enthusiastic he might head to the nearest table and forcibly grab two or three guests to join the dance.

Soul Food

Animals, plants, star-sprayed nights, adventure, culture and romance are all reason enough to expend the time and money journeying to this remote corner of the world. But why do so many people who earn huge amounts of money wistfully remark that they would love to have my job?

I believe they crave the sense of peace and wonder that Africa has filled them with. Not everyone who journeys here feels this connection. For some, it remains a place of inescapable harshness. For those who return time and again or those in whose memory it lingers, Africa is a setting with which their souls feel a connection.

Africa can bring a tremendous peace to the tired and overwrought soul, irrespective of the season. October is a particular favourite; the early summer before the real heat and heavy rain:

A lion calls for the last time as the cool dawn is broken by the sun peering over the horizon. The grass is newly flushed after the first rains of the season. A pair of Wahlberg's Eagles, just returned from northern Africa, take off as the air begins to warm. The first dung beetle of the season helicopters towards a newly deposited pile of elephant dung, steaming in the cool of the morning. The birds are commencing the business of procreation and there is an overwhelming chorus of little pharynxes in full song as territories are established and mates courted. A herd of impala warms in the early rays, relieved to have survived another night unscathed.

As the heat intensifies, the sounds diminish and by noon the bush, except for the insects, is lethargic, waiting out the heat. In the distance a Yellow-fronted Tinkerbird calls, 'tink, tink, tink', on the banks of a dry lowveld river, a cicada (also feeling amorous after years of celibacy underground) shrills in a Mopane tree while above him a small swarm of stingless bees is busily delivering nectar and pollen to their tree-hole nest. A wildebeest bull flicks his tail at a fly as he dozes in the shade of his favourite Jacket Plum tree. A troop of baboons rests high in a Jackal-berry tree. They snooze, scratch the odd itch, and perhaps pick a fruit to nibble. The lazy serenity is tangible.

The heat dissipates as the afternoon draws to a close. In the middle of a mopane forest the new season's flush turns gold, olive and red as the sun arcs west. A spicy hint rises in the air. As the sun dips further, the storm clouds build over the Drakensberg. The horizon turns cherry red and ginger rays shoot out across the sky. The bird chorus begins afresh as the light fades, filling the evening with cheerful song. When night finally falls, a new refrain of crickets and frogs replaces that of the birds. A lion wakes, stands and stretches. He wanders over to his dozing brother and rubs his face against his flank. The two move off lazily into the gathering darkness.

There is something about a wild African place that the soul recalls from our human prehistory. I believe the peace we derive from being here is linked to our ancient beginnings. Perhaps it is the recognition of this, even if it is subconscious, that brings people back to Africa. This is why Africa is important, I think. It is a small part of each of us.

Nomenclature

Every described living creature has a scientific or Latin name. The reason for this is simple: some animals, plants, birds or other living things are known by more than one common name. Sometimes there are numerous English names for the same creature, sometimes there are no English names for an organism. The same problems exist for common names in other languages. Sometimes a different problem arises: the same name can be used to describe a number of different organisms.

These vagaries are unacceptable to biologists who need to know exactly what animal a person is talking, or has written, about.

A little over two hundred and fifty years ago, a Swedish naturalist, Carolus Linnaeus, recognised this problem and introduced the binomial system of classification, which has been the only enduring solution to the dilemma of naming living things. He used Latin because that was the universal language of science at the time.

For instance, the scientific binomial for the lion is *Panthera leo*. *Panthera* is the genus name and *leo* is the species name. The leopard is a close relative of the lion and this is reflected in its Latin name: *Panthera pardus* (which illustrates its relatedness by placing it in the same genus as the lion).

In this book we have used common names because, for the species written about, they are the names that most readers will be familiar with. To avoid confusion, when we refer to names of more than two words in the book (whether bird, plant, animal or other) we have used capital letters. For example: African Hawk-Eagle, Red Lechwe or Large Fever-berry all refer to specific species. After that, the creature is often referred to by its 'generic' name. So the above terms become: hawk-eagle, lechwe and fever-berry. Specific names that are only one word long – like lion or marula – are treated as generics and written in the lower case.

What follows is a list of scientific names for all the species mentioned in this book. This is to obviate any confusion for readers interested in the exact identity of the creatures we have written about. Although, in most cases, this may seem obvious, there are many instances where confusion can arise. For example, the predatory African buzzards are very different from the North American scavenger that may also be referred to as a buzzard. Likewise, the leopard referred to in our text is not the same as the Snow Leopard of Asia, nor is it a close relative of the Clouded Leopard of that continent.

MAMMALS

Aardwolf	*Proteles cristatus*
African Buffalo	*Syncerus caffer*
African Elephant	*Loxodonta africana*
African Wild Dog	*Lycaon pictus*
Bat-eared Fox	*Otocyon megalotis*
Burchell's Zebra	*Equus burchelli*
Bushbuck	*Tragelaphus scriptus*
Bushveld Gerbil	*Tatera leucogaster*
Black-backed Jackal	*Canis mesomelas*
Black Rhino	*Diceros bicornis*
Blue Wildebeest	*Connochaetes taurinus*
Chacma Baboon	*Papio cynocephalus*
Cheetah	*Acinonynx jubatus*
Common Reedbuck	*Redunca arundinum*
Common Waterbuck	*Kobus ellipsiprymnus*
Gemsbok	*Oryx gazella*
Giraffe	*Giraffa camelopardalis*
Greater Kudu	*Tragelaphus strepsiceros*
Hartmann's Mountain Zebra	*Equus zebra hartmannae*
Hippopotamus	*Hippopotamus amphibius*
Honey Badger	*Mellivora capensis*
Impala	*Aepyceros melampus*
Large-spotted Genet	*Genetta tigrina*
Leopard	*Panthera pardus*
Lion	*Panthera leo*
Meerkat (Suricate)	*Suricata suricatta*
Nyala	*Tragelaphus angasii*
Oribi	*Ourebia ourebi*
Porcupine	*Hystrix africaeaustralis*
Red Lechwe	*Kobus leche*
Scrub Hare	*Lepus saxatilis*

Serval	*Leptailurus serval*
Sitatunga	*Tragelaphus spekei*
Small-spotted Cat	*Felis nigripes*
Small-spotted Genet	*Genetta genetta*
Spotted Hyaena	*Crocuta crocuta*
Springbok	*Antidorcas marsupialis*
Steenbok	*Raphicerus campestris*
Thick-tailed Bushbaby	*Otolemur crassicaudatus*
Tiger	*Panthera tigris*
Tree Squirrel	*Paraxerus cepapi*
Tsessebe	*Damaliscus lunatus*
Vervet Monkey	*Cercopithecus aethiops*
Warthog	*Phacochoerus africanus*
White Rhino	*Ceratotherium simum*

Notes:

Desert Black Rhinoceros is a term used to describe Black Rhino found in the very arid regions of north-western Namibia. It belongs to a sub-species of Black Rhino, *Diceros bicornis bicornis,* which is also found in the Northern Cape of South Africa and has been translocated to other areas.

Desert Elephant is a term used to describe African Elephant from the north-western parts of Namibia. Elephant in this region have certain features which distinguish them from their counterparts further inland but they are not different enough to warrant the status of 'sub-species'.

BIRDS

African Barred Owlet	*Glaucidium capense*
African Hawk-Eagle	*Aquila fasciatus*
African Scops-Owl	*Otus senegalensis*
African Skimmer	*Rhynchops flavirostris*
African Wood-Owl	*Strix woodfordii*
Arrow-marked Babbler	*Turdoides jardineii*
Barn Owl	*Tyto alba*
Barn Swallow	*Hirundo rustica*
Bearded Woodpecker	*Dendropicos namaquus*
Blue Waxbill	*Uraeginthus angolensis*
Bower birds	(Not found in Africa but members of the Family: Ptilonorhynchidae)
Brown Firefinch	*Lagonosticta nitidula*
Cape Eagle-Owl	*Bubo capensis*
Chinspot Batis	*Batis molitor*
Common Ostrich	*Struthio camelus*
Coppery-tailed Coucal	*Centropus cupreicaudus*
Crested Barbet	*Trachyphonus vaillantii*
Crowned Lapwing	*Vanellus coronatus*
Dark-capped Bulbul	*Pycnonotus tricolor*
Eastern Black-headed Oriole	*Oriolus larvatus*
Eastern Bronze-naped Pigeon	*Columba delegorguei*
European Bee-eater	*Merops apiaster*
Fiery-necked Nightjar	*Caprimulgus pectoralis*
Grass Owl	*Tyto capensis*
Green Wood-Hoopoe	*Phoeniculus purpureus*
Grey-headed Bush-Shrike	*Malaconotus blanchoti*
Hamerkop	*Scopus umbretta*
Hartaub's Babbler	*Turdoides hartlaubii*
Helmeted Guineafowl	*Numida meleagris*
Hooded Vulture	*Necrosyrtes monachus*

Levaillant's Cuckoo	*Oxylophus levaillantii*
Little Sparrowhawk	*Accipiter minullus*
Long-toed Lapwing	*Vanellus crassirostris*
Marsh Owl	*Asio capensis*
Martial Eagle	*Polemaetus bellicosus*
Natal Francolin	*Pternistes natalensis*
Olive Woodpecker	*Dendropicos griseocephalus*
Pearl-spotted Owlet	*Glaucidium perlatum*
Pel's Fishing-Owl	*Scotopelia peli*
Peregrine Falcon	*Falco peregrinus*
Red-billed Hornbill	*Tockus erythrorhynchus*
Red-crested Korhaan	*Eupodotis ruficrista*
Retz's Helmet-Shrike	*Prionops retzii*
Rock Dove	*Columba livia*
Rudd's Apalis	*Apalis ruddi*
Rufous-naped Lark	*Mirafra africana*
Sabota Lark	*Calendulauda sabota*
Spotted Eagle-Owl	*Bubo africanus*
Southern Carmine Bee-eater	*Merops nubicoides*
Southern Grey-headed Sparrow	*Passer diffusus*
Southern Ground-Hornbill	*Bucorvus leadbeateri*
Southern White-faced Scops-Owl	*Ptilopsus granti*
Southern Yellow-billed Hornbill	*Tockus leucomelas*
Steppe Eagle	*Aquila nipalensis*
Striped Kingfisher	*Halcyon chelicuti*
Swainson's Spurfowl	*Pternistes swainsonii*
Swamp Boubou	*Laniarus aethiopicus*
Verreaux's Eagle-Owl	*Bubo lacteus*
Violet-backed Starling	*Cinnyricinclus leucogaster*
Violet Wood-Hoopoe	*Phoeniculus damarensis*
Wahlberg's Eagle	*Aquila wahlbergi*
Western Banded Snake-Eagle	*Circaetus cinerascens*
White-browed Scrub-Robin	*Cercotrichas leucophrys*
White-crested Helmet-Shrike	*Prionops plumatus*

Willow Warbler	*Phylloscopus trochilus*
Woodland Kingfisher	*Halcyon senegalensis*
Yellow-fronted Tinkerbird	*Pogoniulus crysoconus*

REPTILES

Bibron's Burrowing Asp	*Atractaspis bibronii*
Black Mamba	*Dendroaspis polylepis*
Boomslang	*Dispholidus typus*
Eastern Tiger Snake	*Telescopus semiannulatus*
Flap-necked Chameleon	*Chamaeleo dilepsis*
Giant Plated Lizard	*Gerrhosaurus validus*
Mozambique Spitting Cobra	*Naja mossambica*
Nile Crocodile	*Crocodylus niloticus*
Puff Adder	*Bitis arietans*
Red-lipped Snake	*Crotaphopeltis hotamboeia*
Southern African Python	*Python sebae*
Southern Brown House Snake	*Lamprophis capensis*
Spotted Bush Snake	*Philothamnus semivariegatus*

TREES AND OTHER PLANTS

African Mangosteen	*Garcinia livingstonei*
Ana Tree	*Faidherbia albida*
Apple Leaf	see 'Rain Tree'
False Marula	*Lannea schweinfurthii*
Flaky Thorn	*Acacia exuvialis*
Jackal-berry	*Diospyros mespiliformis*

Jacket Plum	*Pappea capensis*
Knob Thorn	*Acacia nigrescens*
Lala Palm	*Hyphaene coriacea*
Large Fever-berry	*Croton megalobotrys*
Large-fruited Bushwillow	*Combretum zeyheri*
Leadwood	*Combretum imberbe*
Marula	*Sclerocarya birrea*
Magic guarri	*Euclea divinorum*
Mopane	*Colophospermum mopane*
Natal Mahogany	*Trichilia emetica*
Papyrus	*Cyperus papyrus*
Rain Tree	*Philenoptera violacea*
Silver Cluster-leaf	*Terminalia sericea*
Sycamore Fig	*Ficus sycomorus*
Tamboti	*Spirostachys africana*
Tree Wisteria	*Bolusanthus speciosus*
Weeping Boer-bean	*Schotia brachypetala*
Wild Date Palm	*Phoenix reclinata*
Wild Sage	*Pechuel-loeschea leubnitziae*

INSECTS

African Monarch	*Danaus chrysippus*
Common Diadem	*Hypolimnas misippus*
Elegant Grasshopper	*Zonocerus elegans*
Stingless Bee	*Meliponula* sp.

About the Authors

DAVID HOOD

Pursuing a long-time interest in things natural, David began working at safari lodges after finishing a degree in Zoology and Entomology. After a couple of years in Botswana and travelling the world, he returned to the South African lowveld as a guide. This is where he developed his passion for long walks in the bush, tracking and viewing wildlife on foot. He believes that the best way to view *most* wildlife is on foot. He is particularly interested in the 'little creatures'. David has also guided in Namibia, Tanzania and the Eastern Cape and currently works as a freelance writer.

JAMES HENDRY

James arrived in the bush with no experience – clueless and terrified. He stayed, and spent five years at a lodge in the lowveld, three as head-ranger. He has a special interest in Shangane culture and history and speaks both Shangane and Zulu. He researched the little-known history of the Shangane people in the lowveld areas bordering the Kruger National Park and, leaving his first lodge, was employed as a researcher at Londolozi Game Reserve focusing on the situation of the people surrounding the Sabi-Sand Reserve. He has an Honours degree in Wildlife Science. James is also a musician and dreams of becoming a rock star!

CHRIS ROCHE

An early childhood passion for birdwatching and wild places guided Chris into a career in ecotourism. He cut his teeth with seven years of guiding, guide training and assessment, and ecological consultancy with Conservation Corporation in southern Africa before joining Wilderness Safaris. He is currently based in Johannesburg as an ecologist and communications manager for Wilderness Safaris. He has a Masters degree in Historical Ecology and edits an annual publication that showcases wildlife and sociological research in private concessions across east and southern Africa.

MEGAN EMMETT

Megan Emmett is a Nature Conservation graduate who spends most of her time researching and writing for wildlife documentaries. She worked as a field guide in numerous different regions and parks, including two and a half years in the lowveld. Megan works as a freelance environmental journalist and trains field guides in Ecotourism. Megan's work is rooted in a deep appreciation of African wilderness.